IMAGES
of America

SAN ANTONIO'S HISTORIC HOTELS

The US Army surrenders on February 16, 1861. Sitting on the north side of Main Plaza, the Plaza House opened in 1845 and would later become one of the city's first two-story buildings. Gov. Sam Houston stayed at the hotel when he came to rally support to stay in the Union. Ironically, the next year, Maj. Gen. David Twiggs surrendered his Federal troops and command stationed in Texas to Col. Ben McCullough of the Texas Cavalry at the beginning of the Civil War. McCullough successfully sent about 90 men into San Antonio before dawn to stand guard and then led roughly 500 volunteers to seize the Federal properties and munitions for the Confederacy. (Courtesy of the Daughters of the Republic of Texas Collection at Texas A&M University–San Antonio.)

On the Cover: In a nostalgic moment, two guests enjoy the fruits of traveling with a soda pop on the Menger Hotel patio. There are so many personal and historical stories that can be shared about the Menger Hotel as well as the other hotels featured here. This book attempts to take the reader on a journey and invoke thought and appreciation by bringing to light photographs, ephemera, and history rarely revealed about San Antonio's historic hotels. (Courtesy of Ernesto L. Malacara.)

IMAGES
of America

SAN ANTONIO'S HISTORIC HOTELS

David L. Peché
Foreword by Henry Cisneros

ARCADIA
PUBLISHING

ISBN 978-1-4671-0247-6

Published by Arcadia Publishing
Charleston, South Carolina

Printed in the United States of America

Library of Congress Control Number: 2018941270

For all general information, please contact Arcadia Publishing:
Telephone 843-853-2070
Fax 843-853-0044
E-mail sales@arcadiapublishing.com
For customer service and orders:
Toll-Free 1-888-313-2665

Visit us on the Internet at www.arcadiapublishing.com

This book is dedicated to my parents for the gifts of education, travel, and history that now allow me to present this gift to this city I love.

Contents

ACKNOWLEDGMENTS

My respect and appreciation go to all the photographers who documented San Antonio's rich history, such as Henry A. Doerr, Samuel E. Jacobson, F. Hardesty, Harvey Patterson, and Eugene O. Goldbeck. A special thank-you to Ernst Raba, whose work inspired me to go out and create something unique. I give thanks to my mom and dad for allowing me to use a camera at eight years old. That I continue to put forth my best effort is a reflection of their guidance to become a caring, giving son. Thank you Edna Campos Gravenhorst for helping me start this book. I thank my friend, fellow historian, and professional photographer Raul Medina III, who also helped with my first book. Thank you to fellow Central Catholic alumnus and professional photographer Al Rendon. Your work documenting our city invigorated my creativity. Thank you Norma Bressin for your help. Paulette Berger, cheers for your support and help at Camera Exchange. Thank you to my friend, mentor, and professional photographer Jim Landers; I truly appreciate your kindness and support. I thank my friend Chris Rodgers for helping me spread the love of God through Jesus Christ. Thank you Liz Gurley and Stacia Bannerman at Arcadia. Mickie Tencza, thank you again for your help on this second book. This gift could not have truly succeeded without your professional writing skills. Debbie Gonzales and Jimmy Gonzales, your help and expertise of the Gunter and the St. Anthony have been invaluable to my research. To my sister, Chris Peché, thank you for helping me care for mom and dad. My thanks and love to Geraldine Sakellarides for your support through this journey. Holly McDuffie, thanks for your writing help and friendship. Tom Shelton, thank you for your help! A special thank-you to Henry Cisneros for writing the foreword. Thank you to William "Guillermo" Garza for kindness, support, and for sharing some of San Antonio's rich history. I end with thanking the historians from our past who helped me uncover the clues hidden within their books and all the current historians still writing, saving, and sharing our rich history. Future historians, I hope this book will inspire you to research and share our rich history. "A man may only have one life, but history may remember you forever."

Unless otherwise credited, all photographs were taken by the author or are from the collection of the author. Several images throughout the book include QR codes. Scan these codes with a smartphone camera to be taken to websites with video or other additional information.

FOREWORD

There are many phrases over the years that have been offered as expressions of San Antonio's notable charm, appeal, colorfulness, and hospitality. One repeated over decades declares, "Every Texan has two homes: the place where he or she presently lives and San Antonio." Another is attributed to the author Sydney Lanier, who convalesced from tuberculosis in San Antonio: "If peculiarities were quills, San Antonio would be a rare porcupine indeed." Numerous writers and countless visitors describe San Antonio as a romantic experience, as one of the nation's unique cities, and as a city steeped in remembrance of the history it seeks to preserve.

Behind these expressions is a convergence of events, ethnic traditions, and physical gifts that actually does make it special to residents and visitors alike. Historic moments such as the migrations of indigenous people, the explorations of Spanish colonists, the legendary battle of the Alamo, and the birth of military aviation have left visible evidence on the landscape of the city. The cultural legacies of Native Americans; Spaniards and Mexicans; Texian settlers; and immigrants of Irish, Italian, French, Chinese, Indian, Middle Eastern, and German heritages all inspire celebrations, fiestas, parades, cook-offs, festivals, music, religious ceremonies, and solemn remembrances. The regional terrain itself is breathtaking, from the caves of the Edward Aquifer zone to the banks of the San Antonio River that flows from it and from the colonial-era grounds of the five World Heritage Missions to the homes, shops, parks, and amphitheaters carved out of the area's natural limestone.

All of these attributes and many more combine to create a city that its residents treat with pride, even reverence. But it also makes it a memorable place for visitors, who have been known to describe their impressions with phrases such as "a place frozen in time," an "escape" from the frantic pace of 21st-century life, and an oasis of "human scale." These attributes have made San Antonio the Texas city most visited by Texans and by Americans from the other 49 states. It is, in short, a welcoming place of respite, warmth, and hospitality. As such, it is a city with a rich history of interesting hotels. David L. Peché has produced a chronicle of San Antonio's restful treasures and economic magnets—a history of the city's hotels.

From its earliest days as a way station at the junction of cross-country wagon routes, San Antonio's hotels have welcomed weary travelers. Through periods of war and peace, during recessions and expansions, from primitive comforts to modern innovations, San Antonio's hotels have been mainstays of the city's identity and economy. In the modern era, since Hemisfair 1968, the hospitality industry has been a primary underpinning of the city's development. The city's investments in the Riverwalk, the convention center, touristic promotion, the Alamodome, the museums, Sea World and Fiesta Texas, the biomedical complex, the military bases, and other city-wide amenities have pushed the number of visitors to more than 30 million per year. The hotel sector has grown apace, incorporating fabulous new structures as well as adapting legacy buildings. I have often joked to visitors as I tour them through the downtown: "Take a good look at that building because whatever its use has been or its function is today, it will soon be a hotel. If it stands still, it can be converted into a hotel."

David L. Peché has performed an important service by documenting the stories of our grandest hotel properties, offering us photographs never before published, and placing our city's hotels in the proper context of their importance to us all—those of us who live here and those who, thanks in great measure to our hotels, wish they did.

—Henry Cisneros
Mayor, 1981–1989
Secretary of the US Department of Housing and Urban Development, 1993–1997

One

The Menger Hotel

William A. Menger was born on March 15, 1827, in Windecken, Germany. He learned skills needed for brewing and for making the casks and barrels used by the beer and wine industries. In 1847, Menger left Germany for the shores of America, landing in Baltimore, Maryland. From there, he made his way to Texas, arriving in San Antonio sometime around 1848. Menger met Mary B. Guenther, a German widow nine years his junior, in a local boardinghouse. The two were married in 1851. (Courtesy of the San Antonio Conservation Society.)

When the Menger Hotel opened on February 1, 1859, it was an overnight success. It only had 50 rooms and soon found itself with so much business that an addition was constructed in the rear of the building, adding another 50 rooms just seven months later. Today, the Menger has a total of 316 elegant guest rooms, and it celebrates its 160th anniversary in 2019. (Courtesy of the San Antonio Conservation Society.)

Photographer Ernest Raba (1874–1951) came to San Antonio in 1891 from the Bohemia region of the Czech Republic. Having apprenticed as a photographer, he fell in love with the city and opened his own studio on Alamo Plaza by the end of the 1800s. This photograph is one of four Raba took for a Menger Hotel Christmas dinner menu in 1908. The other three photographs were taken in the Palm Court of the Menger, at Mission San Jose, and at Brackenridge Park.

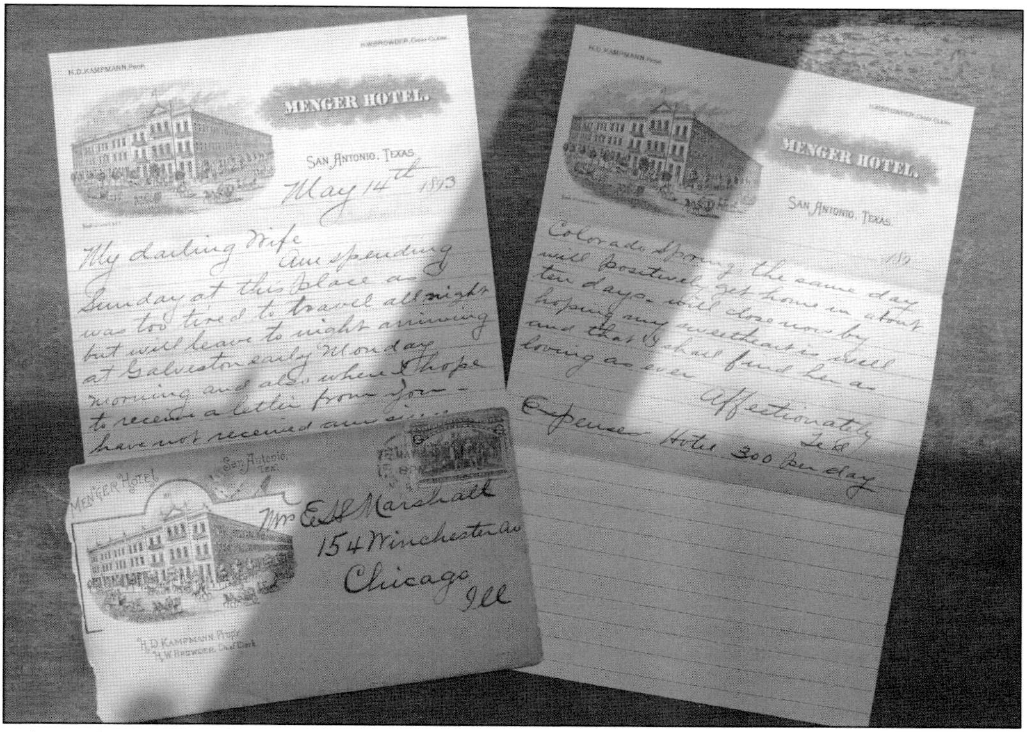

A letter from Ted to "My darling Wife" was written on May 1, 1893. The letter talks about having to stay at the Menger, as he was too tired to travel overnight to Galveston. Ted talks about being blue from the hard rain and the travel delays and hopes to arrive back home in 10 days. He asks his wife to write him in Pueblo, Colorado, care of the post office; in Colorado Springs care of the Antlers Hotel; and in Denver care of the Brown Hotel. The letter ends, "will close now by hoping my sweetheart is well and that I shall find her as loving as ever Affectionately Ted . . . expenses—Hotel 3.00 per day."

A reference to the Menger Hotel is heard in the classic 1957 Walt Disney movie *Old Yeller*, a story about a boy and his dog in the post–Civil War Texas of the 1860s. Burn Sanderson, seeing that the boy, Arliss, loves and needs Yeller more than he does, agrees to trade the dog to Arliss for a horny toad and a home-cooked meal. After the meal Sanderson states, "I haven't ate like

this since the time I splurged on a big feed . . . at the Menger Hotel in San 'Tone." A painting hanging in the old lobby is entitled *Venting Cattle on the Frisco System*. The panoramic painting, of a cowboy roping a steer and two other cowboys on horseback trying to rope another steer, was used in the 1956 movie *Giant*, staring Rock Hudson, Elizabeth Taylor, and James Dean.

A five-page Menger Hotel menu dated June 20, 1949, reads:

> "Teddy" Roosevelt recruiting his famous Rough Riders in the Menger Hotel Bar in 1898. The Rough Riders was the name of the first US. Volunteer Cavalry during the Spanish America War. In 1905, the Rough Riders Association held a reunion in San Antonio that would be the final such meeting in Roosevelt's lifetime. Approximately 50 veterans of the regiment showed up for a chance to re-live the glory days.

Between public appearances on this two-day trip, there was a review of the troops at Fort Sam Houston, a speech in Alamo Plaza, a visit to the old training grounds at Riverside Park, a lunch and private meeting on the second day, and what must have been an emotional farewell later that night at the Menger Hotel.

A hand-colored postcard by the Alamo Chapel shows the Spanish Patio. An advertisement in the May 30, 1919, *San Antonio Evening News* states: "The Spanish Patio of the Menger, Mammy Hahah will be tickling mightily to cook you a chicken dinner that will melt in your mouth. And Over you the Great Palm waves, the roses give of their fragrance, the walls of cool green of fig and mulberry and pomegranate stir in the Gild breeze—and there's music, contentment and good appetite under the stars."

There were balconies under the windows of all the rooms opening to the lovely court, and it was a favorite custom of the ladies to pass the beautiful moonlit evenings on these balconies, listening to the refreshing tinkling of the water and the soft strains of music supplied by a hidden orchestra.

Palm Court "The Menger" San Antonio.

These two-story walls are all that was left of the quarters and offices of the Spanish missionaries. In the 1880s, the walls were incorporated into Grenet's General Store and later into the Hugo-Schmeltzer store. The upper portions of the walls were torn down in 1913.

To the left of the Menger Hotel was the Southwest Texas Immigration Association. The association was composed of one delegate from each of the several counties in Southwest Texas, with its headquarters at the Menger. Its mission was to help those who wished to come to Texas to purchase land, find homes, and develop the resources of the state. The first annual meeting was held in San Antonio on February 5, 1889.

This Spanish scene postcard was inspired by the romance of the patio and the proposals that took place there. In the book *The History and Mystery of the Menger Hotel*, Docia Williams writes, "Once, a guest hired a violinist to come and play sentimental music while he proposed to his sweetheart on this balcony." In gratitude, the guest had a plaque placed on the balcony wall overlooking the patio.

SPANISH SCENE, THE MENGER, SAN ANTONIO, TEXAS.

Pictured is the cover of the 1908 Menger Hotel Christmas menu. The menu also lists the 16 songs the orchestra played in two parts. The first song played was "Uncle Sam's Postman March." A 1908 cylinder recording of that song has just came out and may be heard at www.bit.ly/1908song.

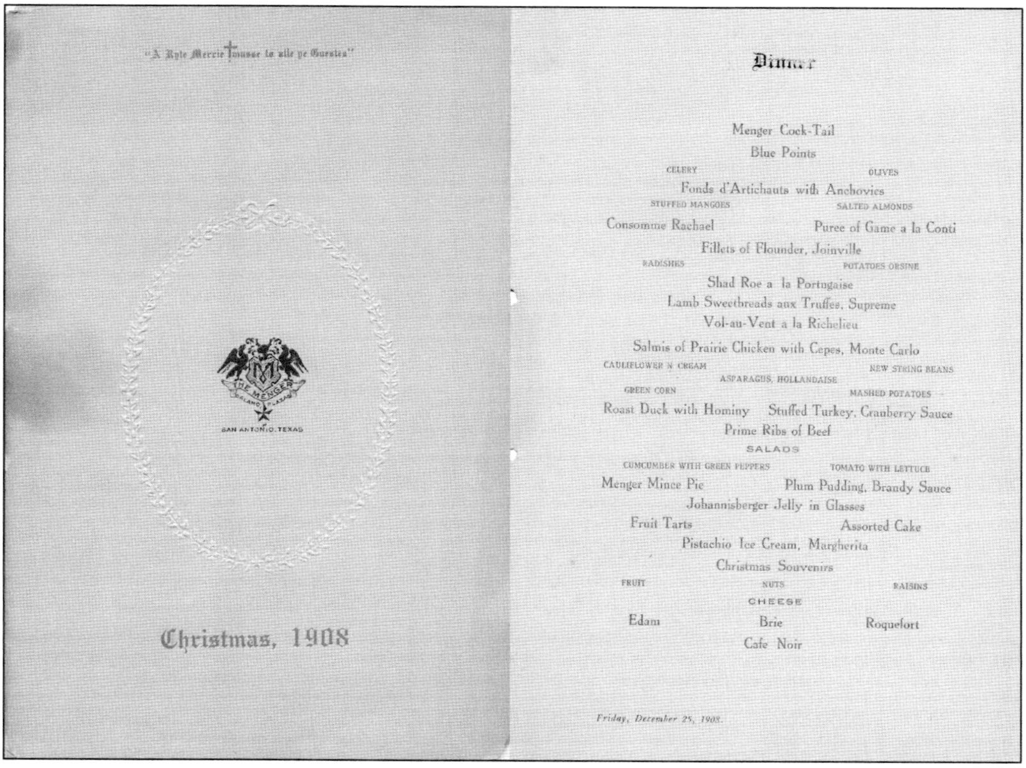

"A Ryte Merrie Xmasse to alle ye Guestes"

THE MENGER

SAN ANTONIO, TEXAS

Christmas, 1908

Dinner

Menger Cock-Tail

Blue Points

CELERY — OLIVES

Fonds d'Artichauts with Anchovies

STUFFED MANGOES — SALTED ALMONDS

Consomme Rachael — Puree of Game a la Conti

Fillets of Flounder, Joinville

RADISHES — POTATOES ORSINE

Shad Roe a la Portugaise

Lamb Sweetbreads aux Truffes, Supreme

Vol-au-Vent a la Richelieu

Salmis of Prairie Chicken with Cepes, Monte Carlo

CAULIFLOWER N CREAM — NEW STRING BEANS

ASPARAGUS, HOLLANDAISE

GREEN CORN — MASHED POTATOES

Roast Duck with Hominy — Stuffed Turkey, Cranberry Sauce

Prime Ribs of Beef

SALADS

CUMCUMBER WITH GREEN PEPPERS — TOMATO WITH LETTUCE

Menger Mince Pie — Plum Pudding, Brandy Sauce

Johannisberger Jelly in Glasses

Fruit Tarts — Assorted Cake

Pistachio Ice Cream, Margherita

Christmas Souvenirs

FRUIT — NUTS — RAISINS

CHEESE

Edam — Brie — Roquefort

Cafe Noir

Friday, December 25, 1908.

This postcard, unused and not dated, shows the dining salon. The Colonial Room Restaurant, as it is now known, was built during the first addition to the original hotel and was remodeled in 1912. The restaurant has welcomed US presidents Ulysses S. Grant, Benjamin Harrison, Theodore Roosevelt, Harry Truman, William Taft, Woodrow Wilson, William McKinley, Dwight D. Eisenhower, Richard Nixon, Lyndon Johnson, George Bush, and Bill Clinton.

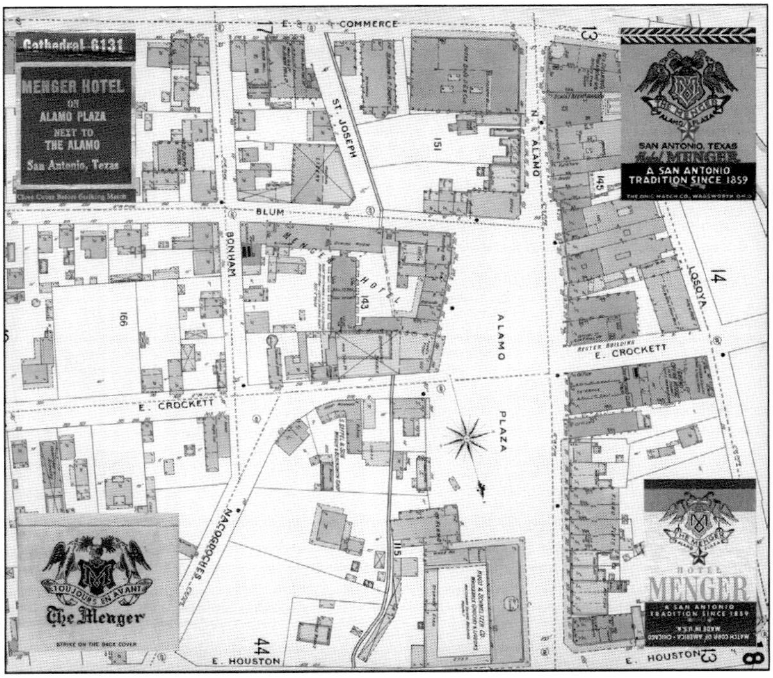

This 1896 map shows Alamo Plaza and the Menger Hotel. Dotted lines where "Hotel" is written show the "covered ditch." This ditch still runs through the Alamo today. There are also four matchbooks on the corner of the map showing design changes, with the oldest (top left) stating, "Military Headquarters for over 75 years." This dates the matchbook to around 1934.

This photograph was published in 1894 for the 72-page book *The City of Missions, San Antonio, Texas*, compiled by Herbert Durand. He writes, "Fronting the east side of Alamo Plaza, it looks out upon the cool and charming little park with its ornate fountain, graceful trees and shrubbery, and blooming masses of flowers." The book was sold at Ed Sachs, the oldest curio store in the city, opposite the Menger Hotel.

Merrill Bishop wrote the poem "The Patio at the Menger Hotel," found in *The History and Mystery of the Menger Hotel*: "Soft, cool breezes from the south / rustle the palms and bend them low / languid the gold fish opens his mouth / and takes the crumbs I gently throw / into the pool, beside my table in the patio. // Listless I play with fork and glass / and keep the rhythm fast and slow, / the violins play. The minutes pass. / And then the moon with silvery glow / shines down upon the patio. // What scenes fair lady moon have met your eyes / in this quaint spot, so many years ago? / When glasses clinked to ladies heaving sighs, / and lips demurely whispered, "yes" or "no," / for romance dwells within the patio." (Photograph by Kurtz.)

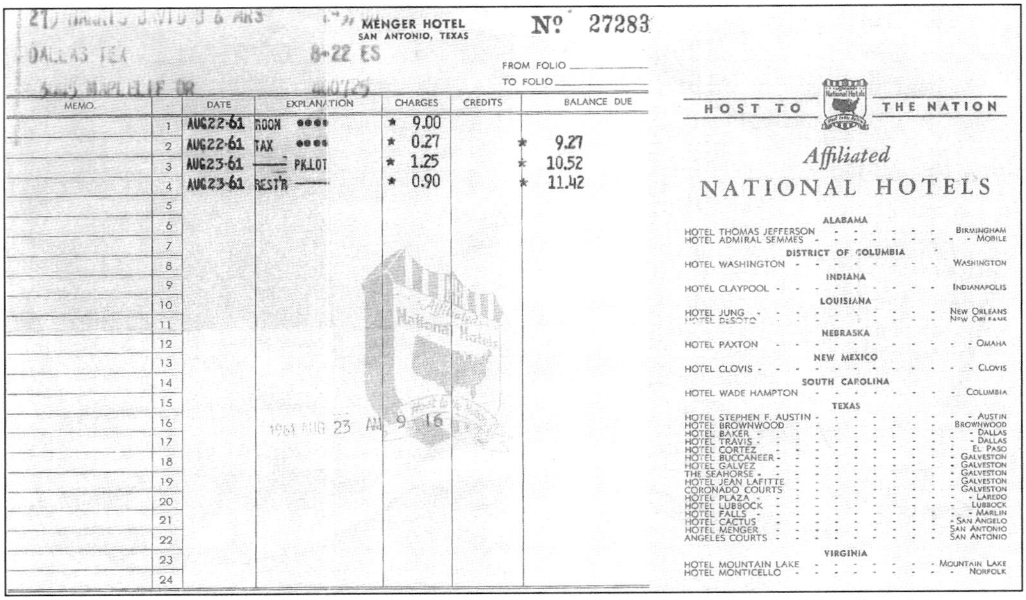

MENGER HOTEL
SAN ANTONIO, TEXAS

Nº 27283

DALLAS TEX

8-22 ES

FROM FOLIO ____
TO FOLIO ____

MEMO.		DATE	EXPLANATION	CHARGES	CREDITS	BALANCE DUE
	1	AUG22-61	ROOM ●●●●	★ 9.00		
	2	AUG22-61	TAX ●●●●	★ 0.27		★ 9.27
	3	AUG23-61	—— PKLOT	★ 1.25		★ 10.52
	4	AUG23-61	REST'R ——	★ 0.90		★ 11.42
	5					
	6					
	7					
	8					
	9					
	10					
	11					
	12					
	13					
	14					
	15					
	16					
	17					
	18					
	19					
	20					
	21					
	22					
	23					
	24					

1961 AUG 23 AM 9 16

HOST TO THE NATION

Affiliated
NATIONAL HOTELS

ALABAMA
HOTEL THOMAS JEFFERSON - Birmingham
HOTEL ADMIRAL SEMMES - Mobile

DISTRICT OF COLUMBIA
HOTEL WASHINGTON - Washington

INDIANA
HOTEL CLAYPOOL - Indianapolis

LOUISIANA
HOTEL JUNG - New Orleans
HOTEL DeSOTO - New Orleans

NEBRASKA
HOTEL PAXTON - Omaha

NEW MEXICO
HOTEL CLOVIS - Clovis

SOUTH CAROLINA
HOTEL WADE HAMPTON - Columbia

TEXAS
HOTEL STEPHEN F. AUSTIN - Austin
HOTEL BROWNWOOD - Brownwood
HOTEL BAKER - Dallas
HOTEL TRAVIS - Dallas
HOTEL CORTEZ - El Paso
HOTEL BUCCANEER - Galveston
HOTEL GALVEZ - Galveston
THE SEAHORSE - Galveston
HOTEL JEAN LAFITTE - Galveston
CORONADO COURTS - Galveston
HOTEL PLAZA - Laredo
HOTEL LUBBOCK - Lubbock
HOTEL FALLS - Marlin
HOTEL CACTUS - San Angelo
HOTEL MENGER - San Antonio
ANGELES COURTS - San Antonio

VIRGINIA
HOTEL MOUNTAIN LAKE - Mountain Lake
HOTEL MONTICELLO - Norfolk

William Lewis Moody Jr. founded the Affiliate National Hotels in the 1930s. The hotel enterprise was one of the greatest chains in the nation. The Menger Hotel and The Angeles Courts were part of this chain. The Angeles Courts had 52 cottages and opened on Sunday, August 5, 1928. (Courtesy of Ernesto Malacara.)

The Chisholm Trail marker commemorates the history of the cattle drives and Texas ranchers. From 1867 to the 1880s, the trail ran from San Antonio up through Oklahoma and into Kansas. Cattle drives would begin around March or April and could take three to four months, depending on various factors. The Menger Hotel was a meeting place for the Old Trail Drivers Association of Texas, established in 1915 to keep the stories and history alive while honoring the trail drivers. (Courtesy of Ernesto Malacara.)

The new Menger Hotel swimming pool opened in 1953, as reported in a story in the *San Antonio Express News*. This postcard view looking north shows the Medical Arts Building, which opened in 1926.

H. Budow published this card. His store at 516½ East Houston Street was listed in the *San Antonio Express News* on December 2, 1911. The store carried postcards, city views, valentines, and fun tricks of all kinds. This card shows the courtyard of the Menger Hotel, which was known to have had a cluster of banana trees, shrubs, palm trees, and tropical plants.

The Menger proudly displays its history throughout the hotel. This display case has various historical items, including a wine glass that was used in the original 1859 restaurant, photographs, postcards, a hotel ledger and guest book, coffee pots, plates, dolls, and awards, all worth seeing in person.

The April 20, 1910, *San Antonio Light and Gazette* reported: "Plans were submitted by Pompeo Coppini to Governor Campbell to remodel the Hugo-Schmeltzer building [left] into a historical museum. The plans included an explanation why the building should not be torn down. The strong wave of commercialism sweeping through our country, destroying everywhere the little that America owned of any quaint and historical importance, which was to stand to our future generations as a landmark of the immense commercial deployment of today." Pompeo Coppini, a local sculptor, would help build the Alamo Cenotaph in 1940.

Two

The St. Anthony Hotel

The St. Anthony Hotel opened in January 1909. A need to expand the hotel was quickly realized, and plans were made for an annex. When it was completed, the St. Anthony was the largest hotel in the city with 425 rooms, had the largest lobby in the Southwest, and with the annex 14 feet higher, was the tallest building in San Antonio. The annex opened on February 1, 1910, marking the first anniversary of the original opening. This photograph is from the February 27, 1910, *San Antonio Light and Gazette*.

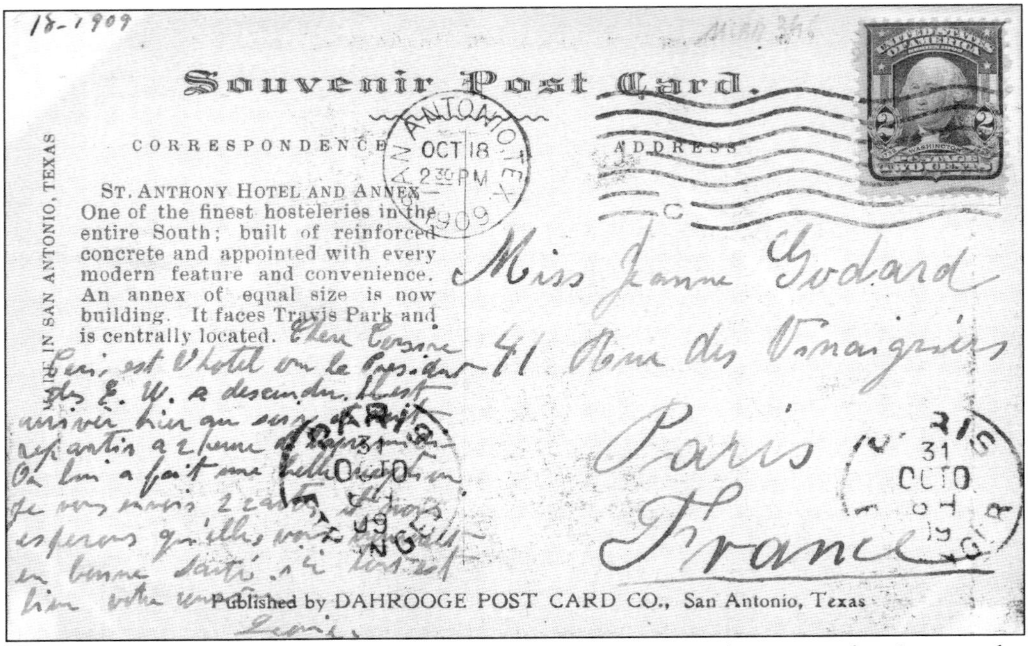

This is one of a 16-postcard collection between two young relatives that started in 1904. "Dear Cousin, This is the hotel where the president of the U.S has stayed. He arrived yesterday night and left at 2 in the afternoon. We organized a beautiful reception for him. I am sending 2 postcards and we hope that they arrive in good health. Here everything is good. Your Léonie" (translated by the International School of San Antonio). Newly inaugurated President Taft came to San Antonio on October 17, 1909, as part of a 55-city tour of the United States. While he was here, he laid the cornerstone and dedicated the new chapel at Fort Sam Houston. The St. Anthony Hotel had the honor to host the president and decorated the outside with flags, bunting, and photographs. (Left, courtesy of the Texana Division, San Antonio Public Libraries.)

President Taft's table was raised 12 inches and set on the east side near the center of the room. The table was banked with "a great profusion of smilax in the center of which was a large white star made of American beauty roses," according to the *San Antonio Light and Gazette*. The menu consisted of Boston pulled bread, pommes duchesse, petit pois française, tomato St. Anthony, basket American surprise, gâteau fantasie, and 1900 Moka and Pommery champagne.

The October 18, 1909, *San Antonio Light and Gazette* captioned this photograph "Where the Taft Luncheon was Held." The St. Anthony Hotel held a luncheon in honor of President Taft with tickets sold at $15. More than 200 people dined in the banquet hall, which was bedecked with rose garlands. After the lunch, President Taft took his station by the door to meet each man and shake his hand as the crowd filed out.

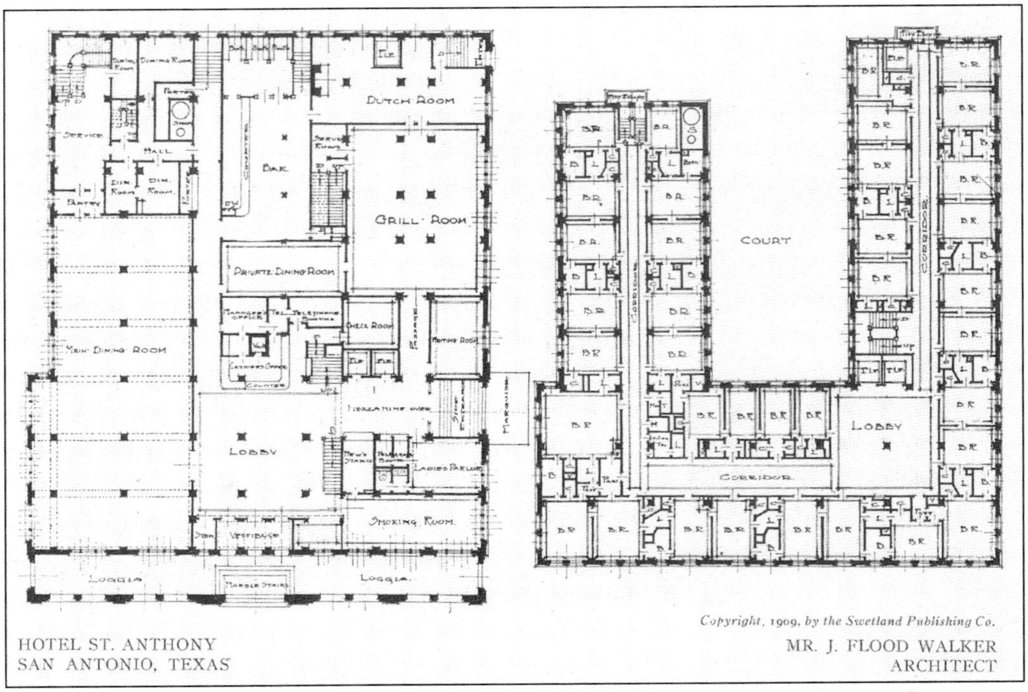

Two draft views show the first floor and bedroom floors. The main entrance stairs were made of Italian marble, and the lobby floor was covered with Venetian mosaic title. A mezzanine looked down on the lobby, as noted in the book *Dusting Off a Legend: The St. Anthony Hotel.*

The hotel's main entrance was known as the loggia (veranda). This entrance was 285 feet long. Countless guests from around the world passed through the front doors, including presidents, generals, governors, athletes, movie stars, religious leaders, authors, and even Princess Grace and Prince Rainier when they visited for the World's Fair in 1968.

This map view of the St. Anthony Hotel shows the heat, light, and ice plant that was located behind the Gunter Hotel. The power plant was connected by a tunnel and was reportedly used by dignitaries and later to move goods. There are stories that the tunnel may have been used during Prohibition, when the Theodore Basher Baker Hotel Company owned the St. Anthony and the Gunter Hotel. (Courtesy of San Antonio City Archives.)

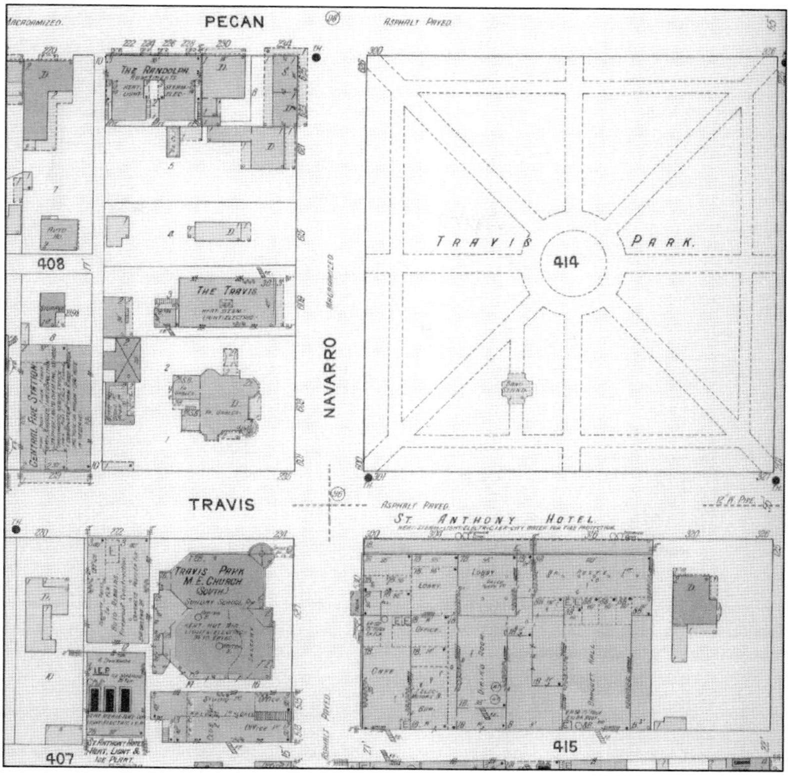

On the night of September 9, 1921, after the city had a day and a half of steady rain, the Olmos Basin topography funneled rampaging waters into the San Antonio River. The only warning came from a continuous blast on the steam whistle at the Alamo Iron Works. The rains stopped around midnight, with 215 lives lost and $19 million in damages. There had been 14 major floods since 1819. (Courtesy of the Texana Division, San Antonio Public Libraries.)

This panoramic photograph by E.O. Goldbeck shows 33 girls, 1 boy, and 64 teenage girls and women sitting at the entrance of the St. Anthony Hotel holding flags. It is reminiscent of patriotic parades staged shortly before and during World War I. The photograph might show Eleanor Brackenridge (top center), who founded the Woman's Club of San Antonio. George W.

Brackenridge was her brother and donated the land that is now Brackenridge Park. Eleanor was also active with the Woman's Christian Temperance Union and became president of the Texas Woman Suffrage Association. In 1919, women were granted the right to vote in Texas. (Courtesy of the Harry Ransom Center, University of Texas at Austin.)

The roof garden café opened in the summer of 1909, and by June 1910, the new eating area spread over the entire roof of the hotel annex and had a seating capacity of 600. There were three firsts: a kitchen that was enclosed with glass so patrons could see their food being cooked, a way to send a request to the orchestra leader to hear a favorite song, and the feeling that one could dine on the "top o' the town," according to the June 15, 1910, *San Antonio Light and Gazette*. The hotel was equipped with nine dining rooms and cafés, including the Old Dutch Room and Rathskeller restaurant. (Courtesy of the Harry Ransom Center, University of Texas at Austin.)

This aerial view shows the St. Anthony Hotel and Travis Park. Above the park, on the next block looking west, is the three-story Travis Hotel. Just above the Travis, the Lanier Hotel is on the corner of Travis and St. Mary's Streets. Across St. Mary's and the river are the first four stories of a building under construction that would make history when it opened in January 1929: the Miliam Building was the first high-rise office building in the United States to install air-conditioning. The 21-story building was also the tallest brick-and-concrete reinforced structure when it was built. (Courtesy of the Texana Division, San Antonio Public Libraries.)

Pictured are a personalized St. Anthony Hotel sugar cube and a room key fob. The sugar is labeled on the back "Crystal Domino Tablets, American Sugar Refining Company." The original 1856 factory was built in New York and became the largest sugar refinery in the world. The key appears to have the letters "WNR" scratched on the back; the letters would later be stamped. William N. Robinson owned the St. Anthony Hotel from around 1923 until sometime before 1934.

On February 22, 1923, the St. Anthony Hotel made history in San Antonio by broadcasting a live dance program over a special wire that ran from the roof to the WOAI broadcasting station blocks away. A powerful microphone gathered all the music and broadcast it over the United States. The special Washington's Birthday radio program started at 11:00 p.m. and was sent out on a wavelength of 360 meters.

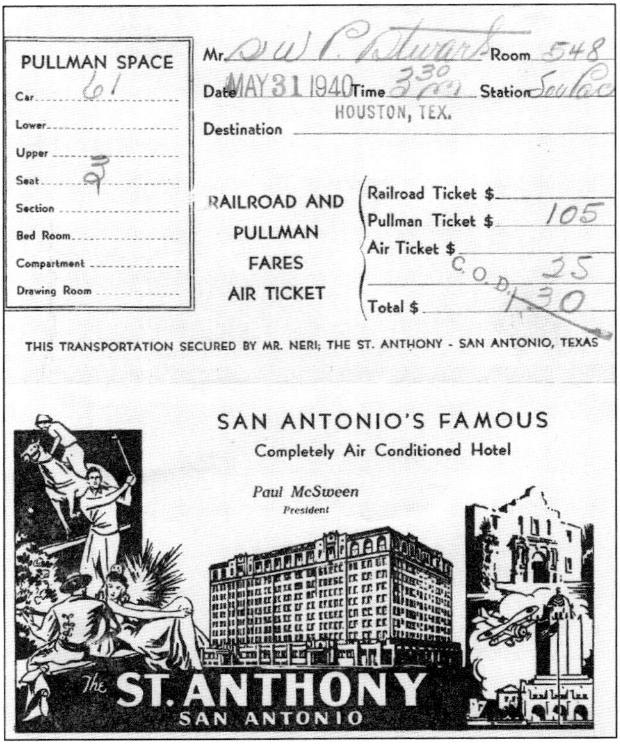
PULLMAN SPACE
Car 61
Lower
Upper
Seat 3
Section
Bed Room
Compartment
Drawing Room
Mr. Room 548
Date MAY 31 1940 Time 3:30 Station
HOUSTON, TEX.
Destination
RAILROAD AND PULLMAN FARES AIR TICKET
Railroad Ticket $
Pullman Ticket $ 105
Air Ticket $
C.O.D. 25
Total $ 130
THIS TRANSPORTATION SECURED BY MR. NERI; THE ST. ANTHONY - SAN ANTONIO, TEXAS
SAN ANTONIO'S FAMOUS
Completely Air Conditioned Hotel
Paul McSween
President
The ST. ANTHONY
SAN ANTONIO

George Pullman designed and manufactured the Pullman sleeping car. The first luxury train car rolled out in 1864 and provided a variety of services: dispatching wires (telegrams), fine cuisine, sewing, turn-down service, and setting up last-minute check-ins or travel updates for the customer. A city ticket office was across the street from the St. Anthony and might have sent runners daily to gather tickets for the hotel's guests.

This staircase led up to the Cavaliers Room, which was established in 1971. During the 1930s, the hotel had a king's suite where the Cavaliers would have their meeting and social events (see page 36). (Courtesy of the Texana Division, San Antonio Public Libraries.)

This view looks west toward the front desk. After major renovations in the 1920s, the hotel was compared to the Waldorf-Astoria in New York City. The San Antonio Cocktail Conference, which started in 2012, has one grand night in its annual conference at the St. Anthony, an event called the "Waldorf on the Prairie." (Courtesy of the Texana Division, San Antonio Public Libraries.)

The St. Anthony Room, Garden Room, and bar are pictured during the 1970s. A restaurant has always been located on the side of the hotel, as seen in the 1909 blueprint on page 26. Initially it was called the Grill Room and Dutch Grill. This area was renovated in 2015 and is now the seafood restaurant Rebelle. (Courtesy of the Texana Division, San Antonio Public Libraries.)

The Rose Shop, located at 1903 San Pedro Avenue, created this bee theme. This two-story Anacacho ballroom was added to the hotel and opened on April 19, 1941. The name came from the Anacacho Mountain Range and the Anacacho Ranch, which was owned by R.W. Morrison, previous owner of the St. Anthony. (Courtesy of Yolix Luna.)

The St. Anthony Club opened on December 12, 1959. The decor was designed by Dorothy Draper and was said to have correlated with the million-dollar remodeling job that was in progress. Decorations and art from England, France, Holland, and India swathed the dining area in tones of white, gold, black, and green. A constant tinkling waterfall behind a statue of Hebe, the Greek goddess of youth, greeted visitors as they entered the private club. (Courtesy of the Texana Division, San Antonio Public Libraries.)

In 1948, Joe Rubin and his father, Irving Rubin, founded the first Joseph's Store in San Antonio. The store grew and moved to two different locations on Houston Street before settling at 233 East Houston Street in April 1970. Joseph's opened two additional stores in North Star Mall and Central Park. It used these window displays in the St. Anthony for advertising the latest fashions. (Courtesy of the Texana Division, San Antonio Public Libraries.)

"Monday, less than 4,000 days from the time we begun, we will have reached a major plateau in our labors. The new 'Peacock Alley,' resplendent with eight crystal chandeliers and twelve oriental rugs, will be completed." This photograph of the chandeliers was used for an advertisement in the February 6, 1966, *San Antonio Express News*. (Courtesy of Ernestine Seik.)

The grand marble staircase to the mezzanine leads to this room honored with the history of the Texas Cavaliers. The Cavaliers were established in 1926 with the goal to "keeping alive the memory of the pioneers, whose courage and daring horsemanship won this wilderness for civilization." They named their first King Antonio in 1927, elected to pay tribute to Alamo heroes and preside over San Antonio Fiesta events. The organization has raised money for charities and has been a positive role model for schoolchildren, the military, and the civilian population during the 10-day city-wide Fiesta celebration. (Courtesy of the Texana Division, San Antonio Public Libraries.)

Three

The Crockett Hotel

A second postcard from the collection of 16 mentioned on page 24, this card is stamped February 28, 1910, has the Odd Fellows Building on the front, and is thought to be one of the first postcards made after the Crockett Hotel opened in 1909. Translated by the International School of San Antonio, it reads, "I am sending you . . . and I will write to you in a few days. Roger must have had a lot to do with all his toys. Please kiss him for us all, as well as . . . Kind regards Léonie." It was sent to Cochinchina, which was a French colony in South Vietnam from 1862 to 1954.

This photograph shows a time when the hotel sign read Hotel Crockett. Research in newspaper archives shows the hotel listed this way in December 1921. The International Order of Odd Fellows bought the land in 1907 and built the lodge hall, opening it as the hotel sometime in 1909. To the left is part of the Bowie Hotel (see page 99). (Courtesy of the Crockett Hotel.)

This eight-page brochure shows the sign still as Hotel Crockett in 1927, when this west wing was added. Also seen is the added seventh story, designed by architect Henry T. Phelps. The brochure reads, "The coffee room colors expressed in decoration of tables, chairs and hangings are orange and blue. Room telephones, ceiling fans and circulating hot water are some of the features of the Crockett Hotel."

The Crockett
HOTEL
Named after David Crockett, hero of San Antonio's historic Alamo.

THE CROCKETT HOTEL

. . . newly reconditioned, offers you every comfort and convenience to make your visit in San Antonio supremely enjoyable.

Located directly across from the new Alamo Park, the CROCKETT is not more than a few short blocks from any downtown business house, yet is far enough away from the heavy traffic noises to insure quiet comfort.

While in San Antonio don't fail to see the many interesting sights in and around the city. Allow us to assist you in planning your tour of the Alamo, the Missions, and the many other historic and educational points of interest.

A friendly hotel in a friendly city. From the moment you walk into the CROCKETT'S large comfortable lobby until the day you reluctantly leave you will feel the warm homelike atmosphere of friendliness for which the CROCKETT is famous.

FEATURES YOU WILL LIKE ABOUT THE CROCKETT

Free parking lot
Beds that invite rest
Friendly, homelike atmosphere
Spacious, attractive lobby
Quiet location

The CROCKETT operates its own coffee shop, serving a wide selection of choice foods, temptingly prepared, at reasonable prices.

RATES
$1.50 to $2.50 Single
$2.00 to $3.50 Double
All With Private Bath

WM. NAGEL,
Manager

This two-page, nine-by-five-and-a-half-inch brochure for the Crockett Hotel shows the rates from $1.50 to $2.50 for singles and $2.00 to $2.50 for doubles with William Nagel as manager. Newspaper archives confirm that Nagel managed the hotel from 1910 until sometime before 1920.

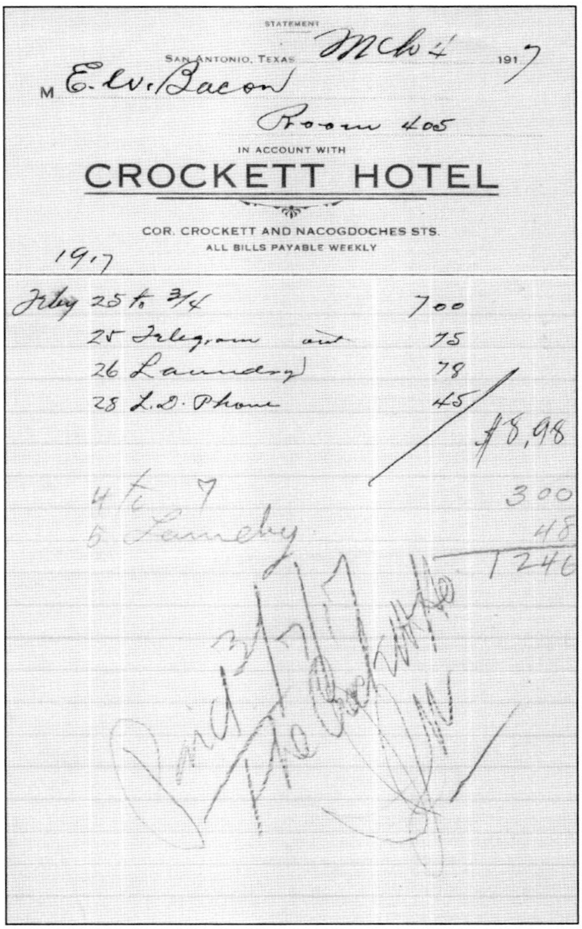
STATEMENT
San Antonio, Texas Mch 4 1917
M E. W. Bacon
Room 405
IN ACCOUNT WITH
CROCKETT HOTEL
COR. CROCKETT AND NACOGDOCHES STS.
ALL BILLS PAYABLE WEEKLY
1917
Feby 25 to 3/4 7 00
25 Telegram out 75
26 Laundry 78
28 L.D. Phone 45
$8,98
4 to 7 3 00
6 Laundry 48
12 46

This bill is from March 4, 1917. A story in the November 6, 1917, *San Antonio Light* reads, "Holdup men are operating in San Antonio. Three bold robberies took place in one night and $68 dollars in cash was secured." On that night, the Crockett Hotel night clerk was threatened by two highwaymen with heavy-caliber pistols and forced to surrender his money, a total of $6. The bandits robbed two more men of cash and a diamond ring, then ran off when three soldiers came toward the hotel.

This photograph came with little to no information and almost never had a chance to see the light of day again. It gives a view of the Crockett Hotel, some neighboring houses in front and back, and a large group of men posing in front. The banner and logo spells "B.R.C of A," short for the Brotherhood of Railroad Carmen of America. It started as a fraternal benefit society and trade

union in 1888 as the Brotherhood of Railway Car Repairers of North America. This photograph shows the Fort Sam Houston Lodge No. 744, possibly after a 1921 Labor Day parade. (Courtesy of the University of Texas–San Antonio Libraries, Special Collections from the Institute of Texan Cultures.)

No information was found with this photograph. There are three movie cameras on a stand filming an event at the Alamo. American and Texas flags stand on the left of the Alamo and decorated crosses are seen in the lower two niches, with the Crockett Hotel in the background. The photograph was taken sometime after 1927; the fire station that was located in the rear on the right doesn't appear. (Courtesy of the Texana Division, San Antonio Public Libraries.)

A view of Alamo Plaza shows the Crockett Hotel overlooking the Alamo. There is no information listed with this photograph, but it is likely from the late 1930s. The two-tone car on the right is likely a 1934 Ford four-door sedan. The Alamo Cenotaph would be placed on the small grass island in 1940.

This c. 1920s postcard for the Crockett was published by Nicolas Tengg. His store was an institution downtown from 1854 to 1964. A story about the store in the *San Antonio Light* on February 7, 1960, read, "World Shut Out. For 25 cents, a customer can buy, *The Consolations of Spinsterhood* printed in 1909. For free, visitors can see a part of San Antonio that has let the rest of the world pass it by."

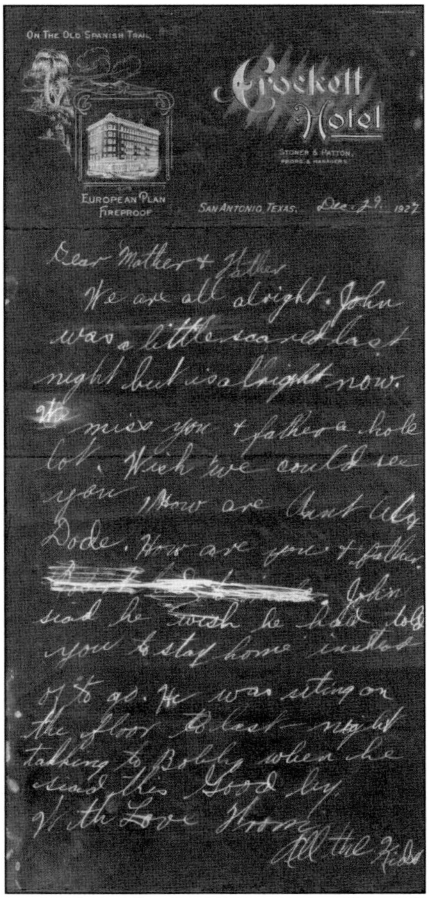
On The Old Spanish Trail

Crockett Hotel

European Plan
Fireproof

San Antonio, Texas, Dec 29 1927

Dear Mother & Father
We are all alright. John was a little scared last night but is alright now. We miss you & father a hole lot. Wish we could see you. How are Aunt [illegible] Dode. How are you & father. John said he wish he had told you to stay home instead of to go. He was siting on the floor to last night talking to Bobby when he said this Good by.
With Love From
All the Kids

In a letter written on paper from the Crockett Hotel and dated December 29, 1927, "All the Kids" wrote to their mother and father that they were doing well and wished they could see them. In the upper left corner is a design for the Old Spanish Trail, whose route goes from St. Augustine, Florida, to San Diego, California. The Old Spanish Trail was still two years away from completion when the letter was composed.

The Crockett Hotel overlooks Alamo Plaza around 1934–1935. Construction on the Alamo grounds includes work being done on the southeast wall. The Arcade, seen with a car driving through it, was constructed with the help of the Works Projects Administration. To the left are the long barracks covered with ivy. This building was used as quarters and offices of the Spanish missionaries in the 1700s.

The back cover of this Crockett Hotel four-page menu was designed for mailing. Prices for breakfast items included 75¢ for one egg any style, with toast and jelly; add ham, bacon or sausage for an extra 50¢. "From Our Broiler," a 10-ounce Sirloin steak, salad, baked potato or fries, hot roll, and butter was $4.75. Soft drinks were 15¢.

Inside the brochure (top left), a message welcomes visitors: "A friendly hotel in a friendly city. From the moment you walk into the Crockett's large comfortable lobby until the day you reluctantly leave you will feel the warm homelike atmosphere of friendliness for which the Crockett is famous." A letter and seven matchbooks show design changes through the years. The matchbook at far right is from around 1927, when the sign on top of the building read "Hotel Crockett."

A soldier sits in Alamo Plaza with a view of the Crockett in the background. Written on the back of this photograph is "received March 28, 1941." This month also saw the completion of the Riverwalk, which was celebrated with a river carnival and night parade. San Antonio's military was ramping up in preparation should it need to join the war. The attack on Pearl Harbor that sent the United States into World War II was to come on December 7, 1941.

This aerial view looks west and at the back of the Crockett in the mid-1980s. The buildings next to the Crockett are the Menger and Joske's department store. The land behind these buildings was cleared for construction of the River Center Mall, which opened in 1988. The mall, now called the Shops at Rivercenter, also saw the development of the 38-story Marriott Hotel. (Courtesy of San Antonio City Archives.)

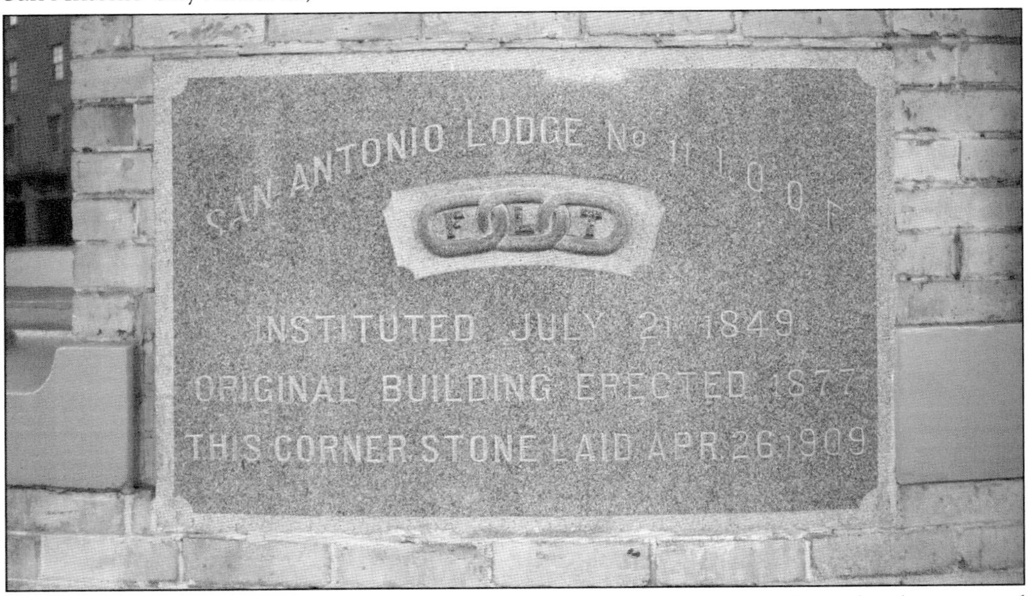

"No Man can be a true Odd Fellow unless he is a good citizen, a loving brother, a kind parent and found in the path which leads him to visit the sick, care for the distressed, lending assistance to those that are in need, and trying to do some good each day of his life." The Independent Order of Odd Fellows (IOOF) was formed in the United States in 1819. This marker outside the Crockett Hotel relates to the photograph showing the original building on page 54.

Rosengren's Book Store started in Chicago in 1919. With the help of Harry Hertzberg, Frank Rosengren moved with his wife, Florence, and son to San Antonio in 1935. After three locations, the store moved in 1959 to the Crockett Hotel. According to Mary Carolyn Hollers George's *Rosengren's Books: An Oasis for Mind and Spirit*, "It was the absolute center of literary culture not only in San Antonio, but in Texas, and was considered one of the finest bookstores between New York and San Francisco." (Courtesy of the Texana Division, San Antonio Public Libraries.)

Henry Cisneros served as mayor of San Antonio from 1981 to 1989. From 1993 to 1997, he served as secretary of Housing and Urban Development. This photograph shows the Cisneros family during the 1984 Battle of Flowers parade. The Battle of Flowers (1891) as well as the Fiesta Flambeau (1948) parades have gone past the Alamo since they both began.

Four

The Gunter Hotel

One of the first hostelries in San Antonio was called the Frontier Inn. It opened in 1837 at the corner of what are now St. Mary's and Houston Streets. In 1851, John and William Vance bought the inn and built this two-story building, which was used as the first military headquarters until 1872. (Courtesy of the Texana Division, San Antonio Public Libraries.)

Proprietor W.G. Tobin advertised: "I have overhauled and completely renovated the Vance House. On October 10, 1872 I will open a first class hotel with all the modern improvements. Bar, billiard room, barber shop and bath house attached. Also, I have a fine stable in connection with the house, where parties travelling with animals can have them well cared for at reasonable rates. On the premises is a fine cistern with 30,000 gallons of water." (Courtesy of the Texana Division, San Antonio Public Libraries.)

This rare real-photo postcard of the Mahncke Hotel garden was sent on June 23, 1899. The hotel opened to the public on March 17, 1887, and had 60 ventilated rooms with well-appointed bathrooms, as listed in the first newspaper advertisement in the *San Antonio Daily Express* on March 19, 1887.

"It is the usual custom for the great hotels of the country to present their guests with a souvenir of some kind," wrote Percy Tyrrell, manager of the Gunter Hotel. This photograph and quote were found in a 36-page book created around 1917 by the Gunter for its guests. This photograph shows the Shriners (established in 1870) passing in front of the Mahncke when they came to march in the Fiesta Parade on April 19, 1907.

The Mahncke Hotel is being demolished sometime around May 1907 to make way for a new hotel. Posters on the wall advertise *The Rollicking Girl* and *Girls of the Streets* playing at the Grand Opera House. The *San Antonio Gazette* published this picture on September 28, 1907. (Courtesy of the Texana Division, San Antonio Public Libraries.)

The book *Gunter Hotel in San Antonio History* tells an important part of the hotel's history. On opening night, November 20, 1909, gold watch fobs and fashionable hatpins bearing a picture of the Gunter Girl were presented as souvenirs to the 382 invited guests at the formal opening banquet. The Gunter Girl watch fob at right was discovered during the author's research, as was the plate, ashtray matchbox holder, matchbook, and Gunter Hotel embossed silver pouring cup.

The Gunter dining room was considered the largest in the South at 51 feet wide by 126 feet long. It had 12 Pompeian pillars, a marble floor, sandstone-finished walls, and a beam ceiling made of oak. Large windows allowed for fresh air and opened to the terrace and garden, and fine draperies added elegance. It could hold 400 to 600 people without crowding.

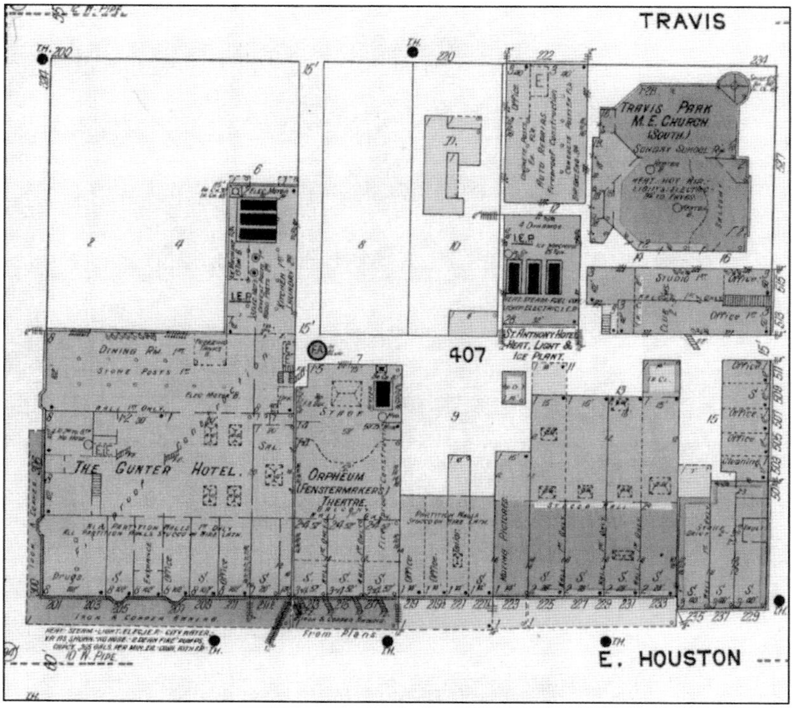

In 2012, the Gunter Hotel director of security, Jimmy Gonzales, helped the author search for drawings and information to find the dining hall. This Sanborn Fire Insurance Map from 1912 shows the dining hall location, entrance, and outline of the first floor. (Courtesy of the Texana Division, San Antonio Public Libraries.)

The December 21, 1908, *San Antonio Gazette* reports that the water supply for the Gunter Hotel would come from a well bored into what was known as the artesian zone.

This view looks east up Houston Street on the left. The photograph, taken sometime in the fall of 1909, shows the Gunter Hotel at top left and the Odd Fellows' original building (1877–1910) just in front. The three-story building at the corner of Houston and Soledad Streets is the Hotel Savoy.

After two weeks of rain, a heavy downpour flooded San Antonio on Wednesday night, December 3, 1914. The second flood in less than 60 days, it was two feet higher than the one that swept through the city on October 2. Sirens sounded, as did whistles around town, giving advance warning. The Gunter Hotel reported that water had flooded its basement, and machinery was temporarily out of order. Luckily, the Gunter had made preparations in anticipation of the flood, though it suffered an estimated $2,500 worth of damages. The pumping and power plants were in danger for several hours, but both services escaped severe damage. Police, firemen, and all available soldiers from Fort Sam Houston worked all night carrying messages and rescuing families.

Information on this panoramic photograph states that it was "likely taken between 1910-1940." It was found in the Eugene O. Goldbeck collection at the Harry Ransom Center. Looking closely at the previous flood photograph, one can see this was taken inside the Gunter Hotel. To date the image and describe the moment, the author combed through his research and found a hotel menu in his collection. The Norfolk Light Artillery Blues of the Virginia National Guard spent

eight and a half months at Camp Wilson in San Antonio in response to Pres. Woodrow Wilson's call for National Guardsmen to assist in the Mexican Punitive Expedition against Pancho Villa. The Gunter Hotel hosted the Norfolk Light Artillery Blues' 89th annual banquet on February 22, 1917. (Courtesy of the Harry Ransom Center, University of Texas at Austin.)

One of the most disastrous floods happened on September 9, 1921. The flood swept an area two miles wide and six miles long. The Gunter Hotel stated that the water had almost risen to the mezzanine. People were caught unawares, as floodwaters started shortly after midnight. This flood led to the building of Olmos Dam.

The Gunter barbershop has been operating continuously since the Gunter opened. It was first mentioned in a newspaper story of December 21, 1908, as being built in the basement along with a billiard room. The back of this postcard lists that there were 30 employees, 18 chairs, 5 manicurists, telephones at each chair, circulating ice water, and all-night service.

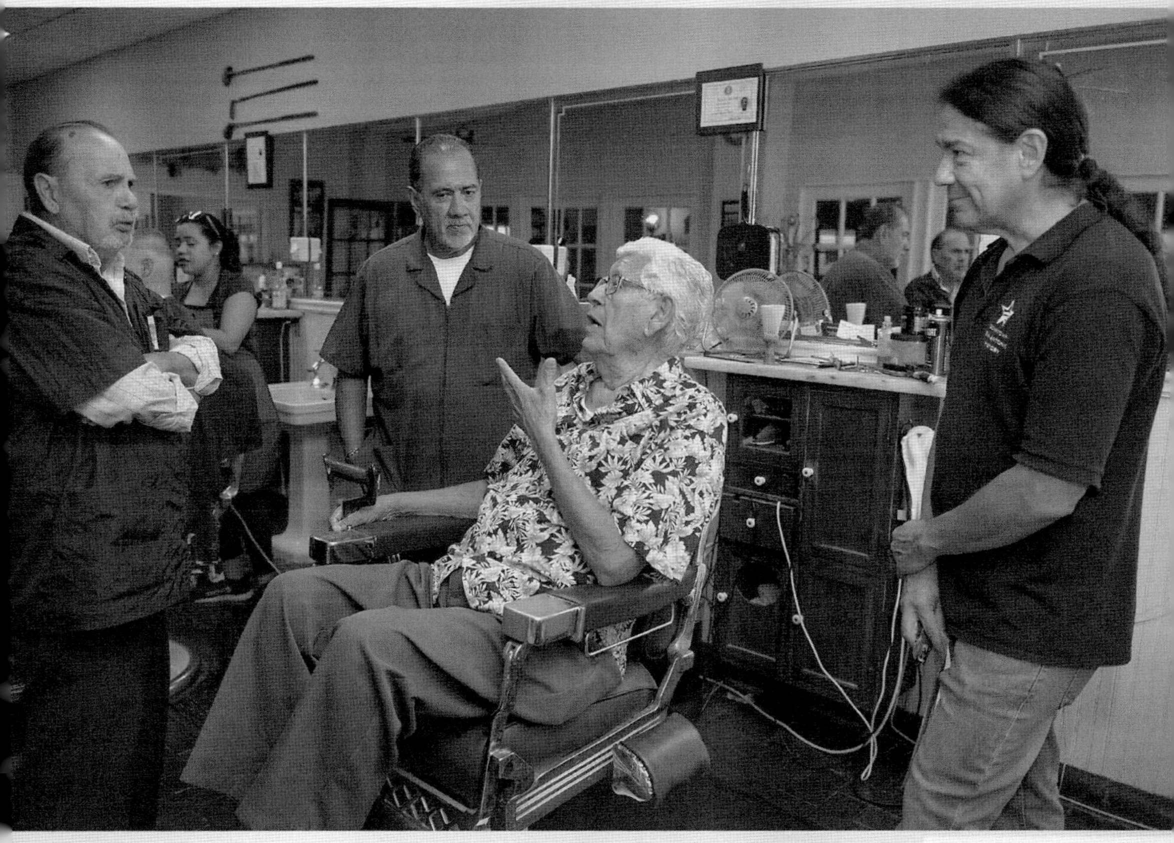

The Gunter Hotel Barber Shop

Since 1909

Just finished having a shave, Manuel M. Peché discusses world events with Lee Bosman (left) and Manny (right). Lee has been making men look their best since he took over the shop in 1975. "I have seen so many changes," he recalls. Manny has been working there since 1989. Michelle, just behind them, is part of the new generation of barbers. (Photograph by Norma Bressi.)

The only information on the back of this photograph is "KU 48810 San Antonio Texas, Jan 1926." Looking east up Houston Street, the Gunter Building is on the left, followed by the Gunter Hotel, the Princess Theater, and at the very end, the Medical Arts Building, which was four months from being completed. Scaffolding can be seen.

This is the inside cover of a 1941 Gunter Hotel lobby guest book. It measures 20 inches when opened and 11.5 inches high. A list of 59 hotel purveyors and supply houses is found on the back.

This view looking east on Houston Street includes, at top right, two signs above buildings for the Majestic Theater and the Stowers Furniture Store. A story in the *San Antonio Light* on November 5, 1905, reported that the Majestic Theater would open on November 13. Manager G. Oliver Laks said, "The opening bill is made up of very expensive artists. Nine headline acts are seldom seen in any one of the other first class vaudeville theatres. From a violin virtuoso and grand opera to a flavour of the saw dust of the circus."

WCAR was the first AM radio station in San Antonio on September 1, 1922. The call letters changed to KTSA and the station moved from the Plaza Hotel to the Gunter Hotel on October 3, 1937. One historical moment in KTSA happened when it hosted the first and only meeting of H.G. Wells and Orson Wells on October 28, 1940. H.G. Wells wrote the science-fiction novel *War of the Worlds*, and Orson Welles infamously adapted the novel for radio on October 30, 1938. This live broadcast caused widespread panic when listeners came to believe that Martians had invaded Earth.

This view of the Gunter Hotel includes the beautiful building sign for the Majestic Theater and the only store still remaining in 2019, Walgreens Drugstore. The Majestic opened on June 14, 1929, at a cost of $3 million, and had seating for more than 3,700 patrons. It was the largest movie theater in the South and the second largest in the nation. Importantly, it was also the first fully air-conditioned theater in Texas. The marquee advertises the movie *Harvey*, the 1945 Pulitzer Prize–winning play adapted to film, which opened on Saturday, December 30, 1950, and starred James Stewart. (Courtesy of the University of Texas–San Antonio Libraries, Special Collections from the Institute of Texan Cultures.)

"The best and happiest Christmas I ever experienced in my life was right here in San Antonio in 1914," said Percy Tyrrell, manager of the Gunter Hotel, in the December 24, 1920, *San Antonio Evening News*. "That was the first time the big Christmas tree and circus for the kiddies were given in the lobby of the Gunter. There were 400 little tots who had a happy Christmas and that was what gave me so much pleasure, and made the day such a happy one for me." There is a photograph of the Christmas day tradition in 1915 in the staircase leading to the basement of the Gunter Hotel. (Courtesy of the Harry Ransom Center, University of Texas at Austin.)

Gunter Hotel
Japanese Garden
Japanese Tea Garden

In the soft glow of hundreds of lights and colored lanterns, the Japanese Garden restaurant opened on Saturday, May 18, 1918. Kimi E. Jingu, a famous Japanese artist, had sold his work in the Gunter Hotel lobby and came to help set the theme with his skills. On opening night, he stood by the entrance with his wife, Miyoshi (next to the white temple gate, left), and painted tiny landscapes, a boat at sea, and the half-turned face of a geisha girl. Throughout the night, Miyoshi handed them out to the ladies dining. The Jingu family also assisted park commissioner and friend Ray Lambert in the creation of the Japanese Tea Garden in Brackenridge Park. The Jingus were later invited to move into and maintain the garden and operate a teahouse. A house was built, and they raised a family of eight while working there for 25 years. In 1941, after Pearl Harbor, the family was asked to move because of anti-Japanese sentiment and the name changed to the Chinese Tea Garden. In 1984, Mayor Henry Cisneros had the name changed back in honor of the family who help created it. (Top, courtesy of the Harry Ransom Center, University of Texas at Austin.)

Five

Hemisfair and the Riverwalk

This view shows downtown in the 1940s. At bottom left is the corner of Alamo and Market Streets. The hotels at this corner were the Jewel Hotel (1910–1930s) and then Villita Hotel until 1967. The A.B. Frank Company building is just below the 31-story Tower Life Building (1929) at top left. In its shadow is the Plaza Hotel, with the Court House just behind it. Looking with a magnifying glass, one can discover buildings along the river and some buildings that are no longer part of the skyline. (Courtesy of the Texana Division, San Antonio Public Libraries.)

The Angelus Hotel opened in late 1905–early 1906. An advertisement in the *San Antonio Express News* on January 19, 1906, reads, "New building, new furnishing throughout, bell and elevator service." Rates per day were $1.00, $1.50 with bath. An advertisement for Casa Rio restaurant, San Antonio's oldest restaurant on the river (since 1946) is visible on the wall. This photograph is dated 1965. (Courtesy of the University of Texas–San Antonio Libraries, Special Collections from the Institute of Texan Cultures.)

The Angelus Hotel is seen in this view looking northeast on Commerce Street. To the left is the "Jewel in the heart of San Antonio" as it peers upwards to the clouds. The cornerstone for St. Joseph's Church was laid in 1868 by a group of San Antonio's German Catholic immigrants, including the Mengers, so they could worship in their own language. The Alamo Street Club was a tavern, and El Diamante Café at 202 South Alamo Street was open 24 hours. (Courtesy of the University of Texas–San Antonio Libraries, Special Collections from the Institute of Texan Cultures.)

Fritz Achtzehn was born to parents of German descent in Eagle Pass, Texas, in 1886. The family moved to San Antonio in 1898, and his father began operating a saloon at South Alamo and South Streets. "It was called the 18 Hotel because *achtzehn* is German for 18," said Fritz, who eventually took over the hotel. The buildings next to 18 Hotel were the Stoltz Hotel and the Shamrock Hotel. The photograph is dated 1965; the buildings were razed in 1967. (Courtesy of the University of Texas–San Antonio Libraries, Special Collections from the Institute of Texan Cultures.)

This view is looking east on the corner of Market and Alamo Streets. The first business by the bridge was the Frisky A Go Go Club, featuring "swinging go-go girls who would steam up the glasses of customers," according to *The Light* of January 13, 1967. The Liquors Depot Store straddled both corners. The Villita Hotel was on Alamo Street. These two buildings were razed in February 1967 in preparation for the city's 250th anniversary and the 1968 World's Fair. (Courtesy of the University of Texas–San Antonio Libraries, Special Collections from the Institute of Texan Cultures.)

With the city preparing for the World's Fair and expecting visitors from around the world, hotel space was needed quickly. H.B. Zachry's Construction Corporation took a gamble and used a modular design to complete the 21-story, 496-room Palacio del Rio in seven months. This 300-ton, $250,000 crane lifts one of the prefabricated fully completed rooms. A helicopter rotor blade was used to guide the room into place, which took an average of 15 minutes. On November 4, 1967, room 522 became the first room to be lifted into place. (Courtesy of the Texana Division, San Antonio Public Libraries.)

The modular rooms were fitted with carpet, beds, color televisions and AM/FM radios, furniture and fixtures, and all utility and plumbing connections. The modular construction was the second of its type in the United States, said a Zachry spokesman in a November 4, 1967, *San Antonio Light* newspaper story. (Courtesy of the Texana Division, San Antonio Public Libraries.)

This photograph, taken on March 4, 1968, shows work almost completed on both the Tower of the Americas and the Palacio del Rio hotel. The first World's Fair took place in 1851 in London, England. The city of San Antonio hosted the first World's Fair in the southern half of the United States from April 6 through October 6, 1968. The Tower of the Americas had the highest observation deck in the United States from 1968 to 1996. When it opened to the public on April 11, it was the 16th tallest in the world. The Palacio del Rio hotel was completed in 202 days and opened on March 30, seven days before the fair opened.

Celebrating its 50th anniversary in 2018, the hotel asked everyone to share their story with #HPDR50. The author's first experience visiting the hotel was in 1976 after attending a concert at the Convention Center arena and walking to the hotel, where his brother Albert was a valet.

This small oasis and red bridge were across Alamo Street inside Hemisfair. The Palacio del Rio's rooms were built in two different sizes and five different decoration schemes. In 2011, the Hilton Palacio del Rio went through a $24-million renovation and was reduced from 496 to 485 rooms.

The River Walk Association has been organizing the Christmas lights along the river since 1981. The Hilton also lights up both sides of the hotel. On the Riverwalk side, green lights are used on the left-side balconies, and red lights are used on the right-side balconies. The front of the hotel also changes its lighting design for special days throughout the year. For the Christmas holiday in 2018, a Christmas tree and the word "Love" were displayed.

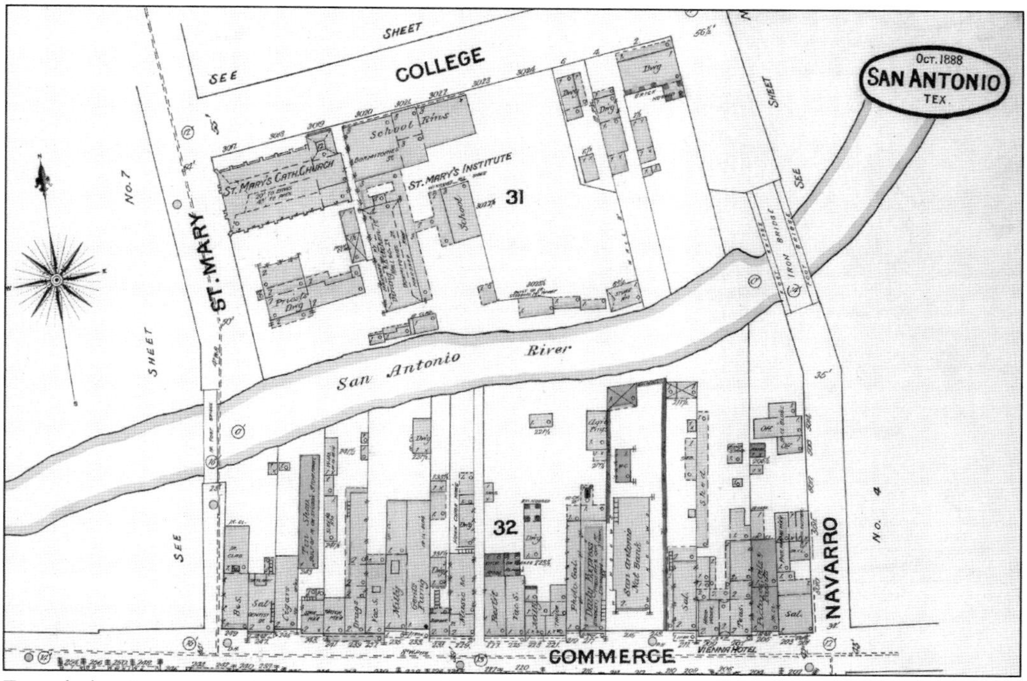

Founded in France in 1818, the Society of Mary grew in the aftermath of the French Revolution's persecutions of the church. Founder William Chaminade focused on reinstilling Christian ideas and values into French culture through education. Four Marianist brothers arrived in San Antonio to establish a school in 1852. After a start on Military Plaza, they began construction of a limestone building on College Street and opened St. Mary's Institute on March 1, 1853. (Courtesy of San Antonio City Archives.)

French architect Francois Giraud designed the new school buildings and these four-story dorms. St. Mary's Institute changed names to St. Mary's College (1893–1923) and St. Mary's Academy (1923–1932). Part of the school became San Antonio Law School in 1927 but changed to St. Mary's University School of Law and Downtown College Law School from 1934 to 1966. There is no date on this photograph, but it is believed to have been taken sometime between 1900 and 1913. (Courtesy of the Marianist Archives, San Antonio.)

"The center building was connected by a porch, and once the playground to St Mary's academy" is all that is listed on this photograph. A young man pushes his boat with two canoes along the river and underneath one of the bridges constructed by the Works Projects Administration between 1938 and 1940. (Courtesy of the Marianist Archives, San Antonio.)

Patrick Kennedy, a graduate of St Mary's Law School, had an epiphany while looking out of the Nix Hospital and down at his alma mater one day in 1966. He told his wife, who was there to deliver their baby, "with the law school moving, the school would be a great place for a hotel with the World's Fair coming." He teamed up with a former student and the builders of La Posada Motor Hotel in Laredo, Texas (opened on July 1, 1961), which had also been a school. A formal opening took place on April 16, 1968, with Mayor W.W. McAllister tossing a key into the river. The grand opening of La Posada Motor Hotel took place on May 19, 1968.

The name of the luxury hotel changed to La Mansion Motor Hotel in April 1971 and finally to La Mansion del Rio, with a newspaper listing appearing in October 1977. The hotel soon won AAA's four-diamond rating for amenities and service. The hotel has 338 luxury guestrooms and a presidential suite on the top floor measuring 1,900 square feet.

Plans for the $5-million El Tropicano Motor Hotel were started in 1960 by R.E. Dumas Milner and his development company. Located at 110 Lexington Avenue, it would become the first major hotel constructed in downtown since 1928 and was the first luxury motor hotel on the San Antonio River when it opened on August 21, 1962. (Courtesy of the University of Texas–San Antonio Libraries, Special Collections from the Institute of Texan Cultures.)

This view looking north on Lexington Avenue shows the small island that was Auditorium Circle behind the Municipal Auditorium, now the Tobin Center. On the left was the John Hancock Mutual Life Insurance Company, which moved to this larger office in October 1956. (Courtesy of the Texana Division, San Antonio Public Libraries.)

The El Tropicano bus was used to ferry all types of groups and organizations in the early days. The retro lobby is filled with color, tropical plants, Mexican artifacts, and three unique spots to drink and dine. A large glass enclosure once housed two toucans named Ricky and Lucy. Out of view to the left was the grocery store Handy Andy. The store opened in 1937 and toward the end was truly the only store downtown until it closed its doors on June 14, 1979. (Courtesy of the Texana Division, San Antonio Public Libraries.)

There are two historic tile murals connected to the El Tropicano hotel. One was a gift to the San Antonio River Foundation from local art historian and author Susan Toomey Frost. Located on the Riverwalk, the San Jose Workshop (1931–1977) mural depicts a Mexican village. The second mural (top left) covers the entire side of the hotel, measuring 58 feet long by 28 feet high, and has more than 313,00 pieces of imported Mexican tile.

The Plaza Hotel advertised as the "finest hotel in the South and the last word in 'Service of Good Living' for San Antonio's visitors and downtown dwellers" when it opened on January 26, 1927. It contained 250 bedrooms that had twin Murphy In-a-Door beds and private baths with both tub and shower. Three high-speed elevators ran from the basement to the various floors. The roof garden was on the 12th floor and was 47 feet by 100 feet long and free of columns. (Courtesy of the University of Texas–San Antonio Libraries, Special Collections from the Institute of Texan Cultures.)

The Fiesta River Parade started in 1941 and is seen passing by the Plaza Hotel. This postcard, postmarked July 13, 1942, shares that the parade did not take place this year, but "Mrs. Allen saw it and it was the most beautiful sight she had ever seen." Fiesta did not take place from 1942 through 1944 due to World War II.

The Plaza Hotel was open from 1927 to 1956 and published various designs and ephemera. It then became the Hilton Hotel until it changed to the Granada Hotel in 1965. In 1968, it became the Granada Homes for those 62 and older. Radio station history happened on February 25, 1928, when KTSA held a formal dedication ceremony in the roof garden. KTSA broadcasted here until it moved to the Gunter Hotel on October 2, 1937.

Snow covers the river bank and an automobile parked on Crockett Street in front of the four-story L. Frank Saddlery building. L. Frank Saddlery started in 1870 on Main Plaza. By 1917, it had branched off into automotive parts, and by 1918, it was the largest saddlery in the world. Before he became president of the United States, Teddy Roosevelt bought a saddle there. Crew from the 1927 film *The Rough Riders*, which premiered in San Antonio, also shopped at the store. Straus-Frank Enterprises still operates today. (Courtesy of the Marianist Archives, San Antonio.)

In 2004, Patrick Kennedy and La Mansión del Rio hotel committed to preserving the culture, history, and period architecture unique to San Antonio and helped open this building as the Watermark Hotel. In September 2010, it became the Mokara Hotel & Spa, the first of a new collection of luxury boutique properties from Omni Hotels & Resorts. The entrance features a display on the building's history. The mokara is a rare orchid with healing prosperities.

Viewed in 1978 from the Tower of the Americas, construction of the Marriott Riverwalk hotel (bottom right) has begun. At bottom left is the west wing of the Henry B. Gonzales Convention Center, built for Hemisfair in 1968 and razed in 2016. The Riverwalk extension eastward is also visible.

The 30-story Marriott Riverwalk hotel is seen under construction along with the Hemisfair tower. The $20-million, 500-room hotel opened in 1979 after a long battle with two other hotel bidders and the City of San Antonio. It would become the eighth-tallest building in the city.

Seen in a view from the Marriott Riverwalk hotel, San Antonio made history when the Nissan Grand Prix came to town in 1987. The author went downtown with his best friend, Michael Trevino, and became part of the estimated 50,000 fans who lined the streets to see the two-day event. Visit http://bit.ly/1987GrandPrix to see more of the 1987 grand prix.

Six

Buildings and Hotels Restored

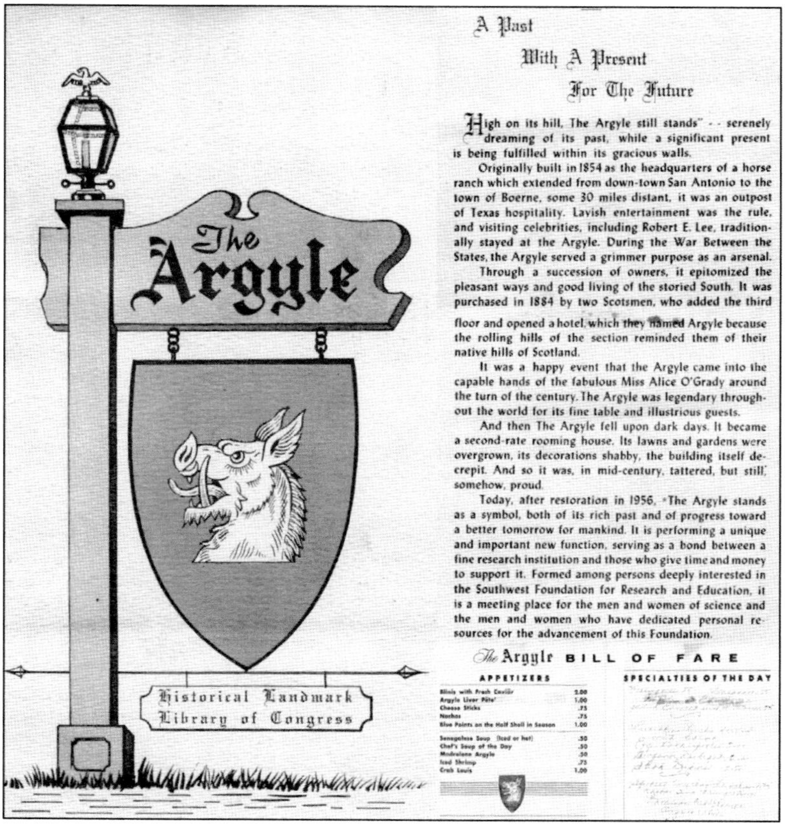

A Past
With A Present
For The Future

High on its hill, The Argyle still stands" - - serenely dreaming of its past, while a significant present is being fulfilled within its gracious walls.

Originally built in 1854 as the headquarters of a horse ranch which extended from down-town San Antonio to the town of Boerne, some 30 miles distant, it was an outpost of Texas hospitality. Lavish entertainment was the rule, and visiting celebrities, including Robert E. Lee, traditionally stayed at the Argyle. During the War Between the States, the Argyle served a grimmer purpose as an arsenal.

Through a succession of owners, it epitomized the pleasant ways and good living of the storied South. It was purchased in 1884 by two Scotsmen, who added the third floor and opened a hotel, which they named Argyle because the rolling hills of the section reminded them of their native hills of Scotland.

It was a happy event that the Argyle came into the capable hands of the fabulous Miss Alice O'Grady around the turn of the century. The Argyle was legendary throughout the world for its fine table and illustrious guests.

And then The Argyle fell upon dark days. It became a second-rate rooming house. Its lawns and gardens were overgrown, its decorations shabby, the building itself decrepit. And so it was, in mid-century, tattered, but still, somehow, proud.

Today, after restoration in 1956, "The Argyle stands as a symbol, both of its rich past and of progress toward a better tomorrow for mankind. It is performing a unique and important new function, serving as a bond between a fine research institution and those who give time and money to support it. Formed among persons deeply interested in the Southwest Foundation for Research and Education, it is a meeting place for the men and women of science and the men and women who have dedicated personal resources for the advancement of this Foundation.

The Argyle BILL OF FARE

APPETIZERS

Blinis with Fresh Caviar	2.00
Argyle Liver Pâté	1.00
Cheese Sticks	.75
Nachos	.75
Blue Points on the Half Shell in Season	1.00
Senegalese Soup (Iced or hot)	.50
Chef's Soup of the Day	.50
Madrelene Argyle	.50
Iced Shrimp	.75
Crab Louis	1.00

SPECIALTIES OF THE DAY

This is a menu from the Argyle Hotel restaurant. Originally built in 1854 as the headquarters of a horse ranch, it was purchased in 1884 by two Scotsmen, who added a third floor and opened a hotel they named Argyle because the rolling hills of the area reminded them of their native Scotland. Today, the Argyle is a private club and devoted exclusively to supporting the life-saving efforts of the Texas Biomedical Research Institute.

This postcard and matchbooks are from the Aurora Apartment Hotel. Named after the goddess of the dawn in Roman mythology, the hotel opened on August 24, 1930. The author's aunt Sally Ramirez worked there as an elevator operator for a short period. She would travel the world as a single woman and inspired the last photograph in this book. (Postcard courtesy of Edna Campos Gravenhorst.)

Alamo National Bank, chartered in 1891, constructed a five-story building at 314 East Commerce Street in 1902. In 1912, when the city widened the street, the building made history when it was moved back 16 feet. The bank announced on January 1, 1929, that this new building would be ready by December 31, 1929. The Great Depression started after the stock market crash in October 1929. (Courtesy of the Drury Plaza Hotel.)

In 1956, the Alamo National Back installed a metal sign and neon sphere that acted as a weather gauge, showing "warmer," "cooler," "no change," and "rain" through its unique lighting design. The bank vault was in the basement and had safety deposit boxes in use until Chase Bank closed this branch in 2017. The photograph was taken on September 30, 2005, when the Drury Hotel chain bought the building and started renovation. (Photograph courtesy of Raul Medina III; key courtesy of Jean Bloomingdale.)

The Drury Plaza was carefully renovated to preserve many of the unique period features, such as stained-glass windows, bronze framework, marble walls, and travertine flooring. The original chandeliers from 1929 have been refurbished and still hang today from the 50-foot ceilings in the main lobby. The lobby was used as a working bank backdrop for the 1994 Disney movie *Blank Check*. (Courtesy of Raul Medina III.)

This rare view from the roof of the Drury Plaza Hotel looks east. The 24-story building is trimmed in granite and marble, terra-cotta embellishments, molded plaster, and decorative bronze. During the 2007 renovation, the rooftop was converted into a pool and observation deck with 360-degree views of the city.

The 13-story Medical Arts Center was completed in April 1926 at a cost of $1.55 million. To its left, construction work is seen on the new post office and federal building that opened to the public on October 11, 1937, at a cost of $2,225,000. Behind the construction is the San Antonio Express News Building, which was dedicated and opened on October 29, 1929—the day the stock market crashed. (Courtesy of the Texana Division, San Antonio Public Libraries.)

During Fiesta week in April 1929, the city used 50,000 colored lights to decorate downtown buildings. The Medical Arts Center used an estimated 1,800 lights to outline the building along with 16 other downtown buildings. The idea originated the year before with Joe J. Nix. The Alamo Cenotaph was created by sculptor Pompeo Coppini and has been a part of Alamo Plaza since it was dedicated on November 11, 1940.

This view looking east on Houston Street shows the Medical Arts Center. The 1950s were a booming time for San Antonio, and everybody came downtown to shop, seek help, and eat. Zales, JC Penney's, and Texas State Optical are still in business today. Neisners is now Towne Place Suites by Marriott, and the Hilton Garden Inn now stands where Florsheim and Payless were located.

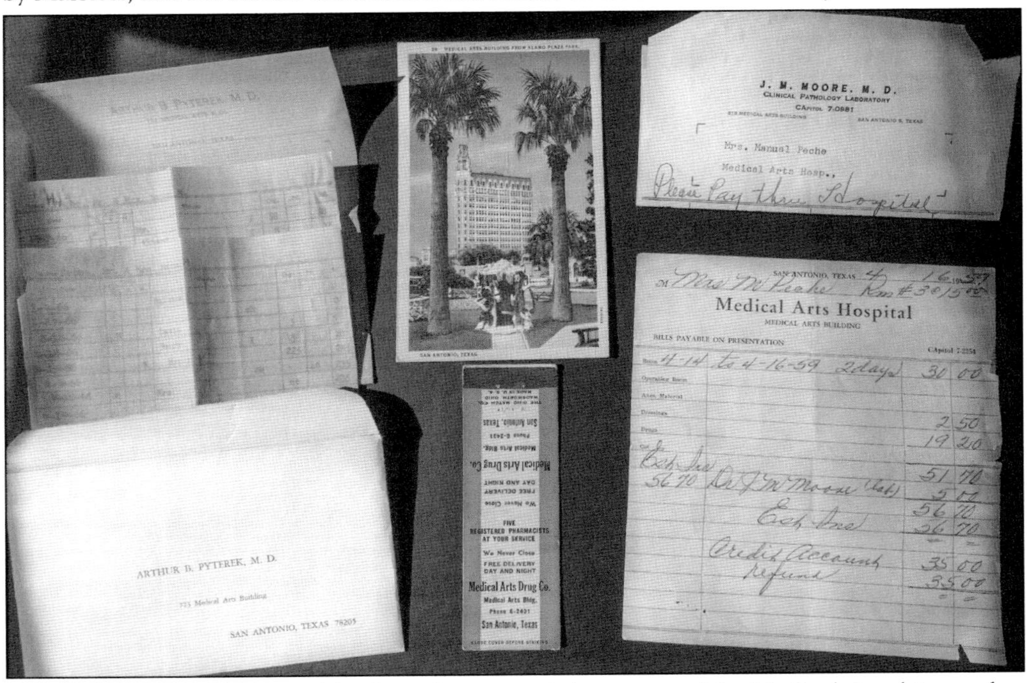

Family doctor records, a matchbook, and a postcard show some of the Medical Arts history that was saved. In 1984, the building was remodeled, involving the demolition and reconstruction of all the internal elements of the building. It opened as the Emily Morgan Hotel and received the San Antonio chapter of American Institute of Architects' prestigious Twenty Five Year Distinguished Building Award in 2010. In 2012, the Emily Morgan Hotel experienced an onslaught of building updates, as it joined the Doubletree by Hilton group and underwent a multi-million-dollar renovation.

The Fairmount Hotel opened in 1906 and was located at 359 East Commerce Street. The hotel charged $2 a day for the American plan and $1 for the European plan. In 1919, the hotel advertised in the *San Antonio Evening News*: "The coolest rooms, lowest rates, free baths, close to Frenchy's restaurant; free sleeping porches for 100 people, rates per week 3 dollars and up." (Courtesy of the Library of Congress.)

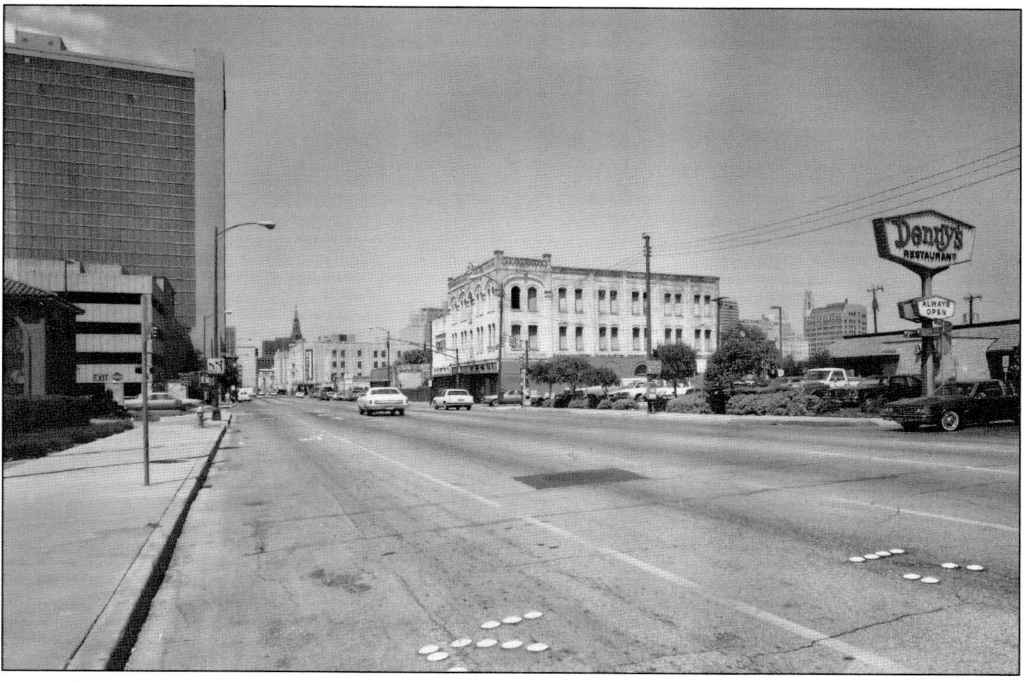

According to the Library of Congress, the Fairmount Hotel is an example of the type of commercial establishments that characterized the prosperity of turn-of-the-century San Antonio. Designed by architect Leo M.J. Deilmann and built by J.P. Haynes, the Fairmount was typical of the buildings that once lined Commerce Street from downtown east to the Southern Pacific Depot. (Courtesy of the Library of Congress.)

The Fairmount was saved from the wrecking ball in 1984 by a group of developers when plans were made for more lodging and retail in this location. In the spring of 1985, the Fairmount Hotel was moved five blocks. It took six days to move the 1,451-ton hotel. (Courtesy of the Texana Division, San Antonio Public Libraries.)

When the Fairmount's journey was over on April 4, 1985, the hotel made history as the heaviest hotel relocated and was honored with an entry in the *Guinness Book of World Records*. After extensive renovation and a new addition, it reopened on September 5, 1986. It is listed as a National Trust Historic Hotel of America.

This view of Houston Street shows the Maverick Bank building (left), which opened in 1886. This photograph, along with 30 others, was published in *Picturesque San Antonio* by S.H. Kress & Company in 1907. In April 1908, tenants in the store opposite the bank were notified to quit the premises so work could begin on an eight-story structure of steel and reinforced concrete.

Farm boy–to–millionaire is the life story of Col. C.C. Gibbs. His climb was marked step by step by hard work backed by the knowledge of when to rise at the knock of opportunity. At the age of 65, he gave San Antonio one of the finest office buildings in the South. Gibbs spared no expense on his building, as he knew it would stand long after he was gone. The building, seen here at upper left, was opened on August 29, 1909.

The Gibbs building has witnessed history on many occasions. On July 24, 1912, thirty-five cars arrived from the Farm and Ranch Tour, which started in Dallas two days before. Only farmers and ranchers were permitted to enter the contest, which was sanctioned by AAA. It was said to be the first of its kind in the world, with prizes of $1,000.

The history of this building, listed as the Havana, dates back to 1914. Edward F. Melcher came to San Antonio at the age of 19 with his close friend Herman Moede. During all of Melcher's 51 years in the city, he followed the wholesale grocery and delicatessen business, selling cheese, sausage, smoked and pickled fish, and a full line of imported canned goods. The house was built to accommodate traveling merchants.

While attending high school downtown, the author would pass this building, which was abandoned and boarded up, and was always curious about its story. Austin hotelier Liz Lambert opened the Havana in 2010. The author and his family were given a grand tour of the hotel weeks after its opening. In 2012, the Havana gave the author and Joan Korte a place to meet while working on their first book for Arcadia Publishing, *Downtown San Antonio*. When the book was published in 2013, the Havana Hotel hosted a book-signing party during the Texas Cavaliers River Parade.

Clockwise from top left are the Washer Building; Main Plaza, the courthouse, and Elliott's Flats; Sommers Drug Store No. 2; a Prudential Café matchbook; and the Prudential Hotel lobby. The Washer Building opened on May 1, 1908. The four-story building had 99 office rooms, with the ground level used for stores. The Prudential Hotel opened in 1921 with 100 rooms. The Prudential Café opened on December 11, 1921. Sometime in 1947, the building was bought and changed to an apartment hotel named after the owner, Morris Kallison. Sommers Drug Store began in 1912 and operated 40 stores in Texas, going out of business in 1977. (Top left, courtesy of Texana Division, San Antonio Public Libraries.)

The 10-story Robert E. Lee Hotel opened on Saturday, May 26, 1923. It was a monument to the aggressive spirit that was fast building San Antonio to its destiny as the acknowledged metropolis of the great Southwest. On opening day, the Gunter Hotel orchestra played, and a beautiful scroll was provided for registering the first day's guests. It was to be framed and hung behind the desk in the lobby to become a part of Texas history. (Courtesy of the Texana Division, San Antonio Public Libraries.)

The Robert E. Lee was built in this location due to several factors, one being the Old Spanish Trail, which passed its corner. At upper right is a hotel menu from December 20, 1937, a key, and letterhead. At center right are a matchbook cover and a photograph of the building before renovation. The new Frost Bank Tower (bottom right) opened to the public on July 1, 2019. (Top left and center, Texana Division, San Antonio Public Libraries.)

With its first class service, the Robert E. Lee helped create countless wonderful memories for visitors from around the world. Sadly, the hotel was witness to troubling news the last years it was open. Two floors were affected by arson, but the suspects were caught. A fire started in one room, possibly caused by a cigarette, ended with a man's death. In a case of homicide, a man was found stabbed and hanging from a shower curtain. In one suicide, a man jumped from the ninth floor.

In 1857, the San Antonio Drug Company had its beginnings in a drugstore established by the Kalteyer family on Military Plaza. About the same time, the Dreiss-Thompson & Co. drugstore was next to Alamo Plaza. The firms consolidated and were incorporated in 1892. The author's grandmother Petra Ramirez worked at this new building during the flood of 1921, and later told how she was called in to help salvage goods in the building the next day. The basement was flooded, and the water rose about six feet above street level. (Courtesy of the San Antonio Conservation Society.)

The San Antonio Drug Company was one of the largest institutions of the city and served Texas, Arizona, New Mexico, Oklahoma, Louisiana, and Mexico before closing in the late 1970s. In January 1997, Homewood Suites by Hilton opened in this building, which is listed in the National Register of Historic Places. In the distance, a view of Main Plaza and the San Fernando Cathedral shows the 24-minute art projection *The Saga*. It was unveiled in 2014 and is shown three times a night, four nights a week. It runs through 2024 and is free.

In 1991, the Neisner building was left abandoned when the Antique Sampler moved into the Goggan building on the opposite end of the block on Broadway. Dale Warren's Wildlife Exhibit, on the fourth floor, also closed. JC Penney's was its neighbor. Stores located across the street through time and up to the Walgreens were Pincus, Stein's, Tawil's, Payless Drugstore, Florsheim Shoes, Zale's, Burt's Shoes, Stuart's, and Franklin's. (Courtesy of the University of Texas–San Antonio Libraries, Special Collections from the Institute of Texan Cultures.)

The former Neisner building was designed by architects Atlee B. and Robert M. Ayres and opened in 1947. It had the second escalator installed in the city. Alamo City Hotels bought the building in 2007. The Parsons architect and engineering firm was in charge of the redevelopment, saving the exterior of red granite and cream-colored limestone and the historic escalator, now the oldest in San Antonio. The building is now the Marriott TownePlace Suites, which opened in 2009.

The seven-story Travelers Hotel advertised that it was open on January 1, 1915, with a roof garden opening on May 17, 1917. The hotel became headquarters to northern and local baseball teams. The Detroit Tigers had their winter headquarters here in 1921 (left). The Piggly Wiggly store opened on June 26, 1918, and was the second in San Antonio. Kelly & Springfield Tire started in 1894 and opened in San Antonio in 1899 (right). (Courtesy of the Texana Division, San Antonio Public Libraries.)

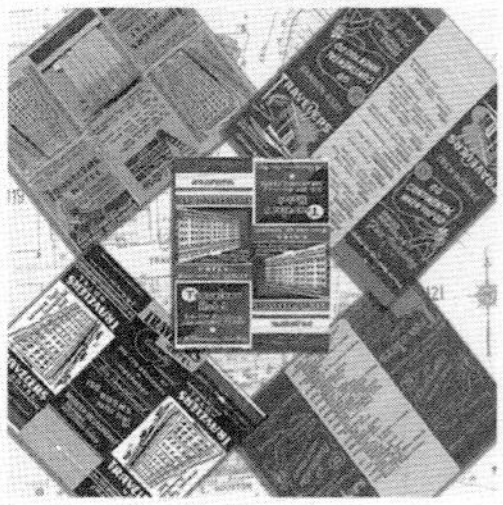

The photograph at bottom right shows the first guest checking out of the Best Western Premier Historic Travelers Hotel in August 2017. At top right is a postcard view of original lobby with the marble front desk still in use today. Local artist and friend Andy Benavides assisted the author in creating the five-matchbook design at center. The real-photo postcard at center right shows a streetcar in front of the hotel going up Avenue C before the street changed to Broadway.

Seven

Lost but Not Forgotten

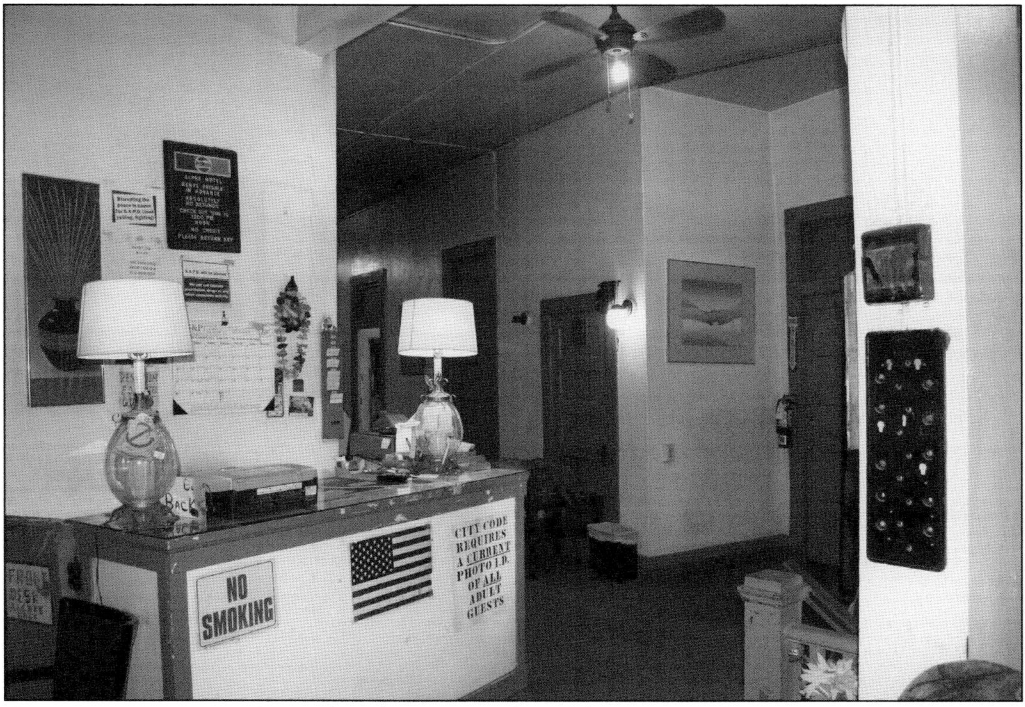

Opening sometime in the mid- to late 1950s, the Alpha Hotel had 12 rooms with weekly and monthly rates from $2 and up. It was located at 315 North Main Street, just behind the Robert E. Lee Hotel. The hotel closed shortly after the author took this photograph on May 29, 2011. It is now the Alpha Center.

The Bexar Hotel was located on Houston Street and started advertising in May 1889 that every room had steam heat, hot and cold running water, and electric lighting. The Bexar changed to the Jefferson Hotel around 1923–1924. The building was razed in 1971. Door hardware and stained glass from the hotel were saved by Kay and Charles Scheer and incorporated in their home at 130 King Williams Street. The house is now the San Antonio Art League museum. (Both bottom images, Texana Division, San Antonio Public Libraries.)

The Blue Bonnet Hotel opened on January 18, 1928, with 220 rooms. The public was invited to opening ceremonies that went from 5:00 to 8:00 p.m. and included music and entertainment. The café also started serving lunch. Radio station KGRC opened the Blue Bonnet Hotel Studio from 10:00 to 12:00 a.m. "GRC" stood for Gene Roth Company; in 1930, the call letters changed to KONO; it is still broadcasting today. The hotel was imploded in 1988.

The Bowie Hotel was located on East Houston Street on the grounds of the Alamo and had 25 apartments. On August 29, 1923, damage to the amount of $2,000 was done to paved streets in downtown after another hard rain. According to the *San Antonio Express* of August 29, 1923, "In an effort to repair the damage as quickly as possible special gangs of workmen assisted the regular repair gangs kept on the city's payroll." (Courtesy of the San Antonio Conservation Society.)

The Cactus Hotel was located at 105½ South Flores Street in the Kallison Building. The small hotel had 50 air-conditioned rooms, with and without bath, and with Beautyrest mattresses and telephones in every room for $7 a week and up. The hotel opened in January 1950 and closed in the late 1970s. Patrons from the Roosevelt bar shared stories of ghosts still on the property.

The new Elite Hotel opened for business on December 9, 1897, with William G. Tobin as the proprietor. The hotel was located in Main Plaza at the corner of Commerce and Soledad Streets. It was advertised for gentlemen exclusively, the only first-class European hotel in Texas, heated by steam and lighted by electricity. The reputation of the Elite restaurant had been established since the late 1880s. Electric cars from all the depots stopped at the door.

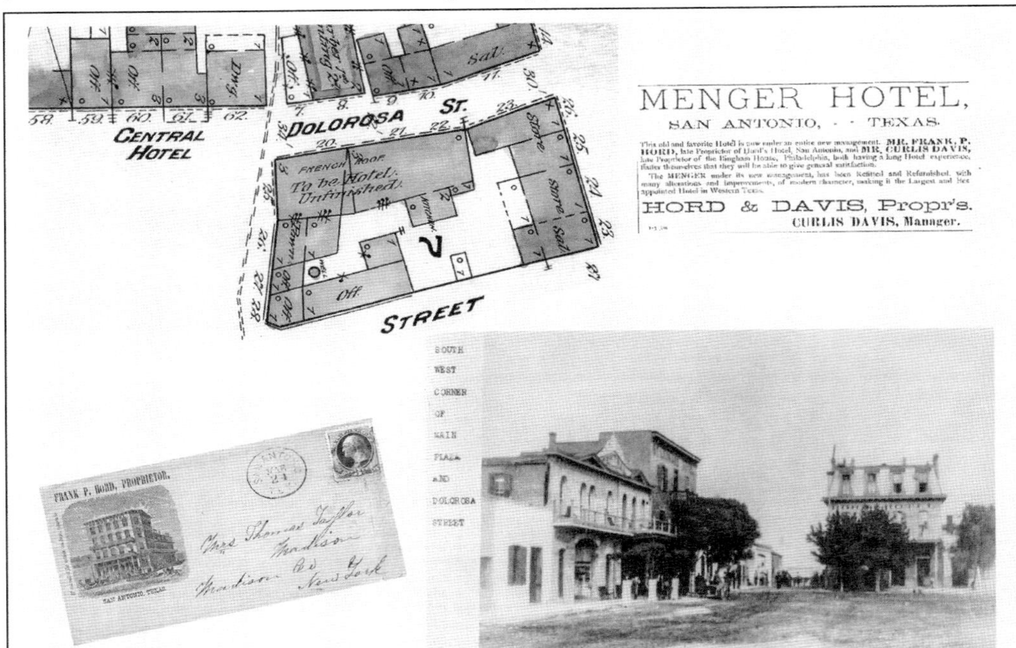

The Hord Hotel opened in the 1870s. A story in the January 19, 1879, *San Antonio Daily Express* reported that a peddler of toy telephones did a good business on Main Plaza by having one of the instruments in operation between the saloon next door and the roof of the Hord Hotel, showing that the telephone had made its way to San Antonio less than three years after it was patented by Alexander Graham Bell. The Hord became the Southern Hotel in 1884. Cornel F.P. Hord went on to briefly manage the Menger Hotel. (Photograph courtesy of the Texana Division, San Antonio Public Libraries.)

The Hot Wells hotel was conceived in 1892 after an artesian well containing sulphur was discovered nearby. Using the resort at Hot Springs, Arkansas, as a model, McClellan Shacklett constructed the hotel, originally advertised as Natural Hot Sulphur Wells. The baths were in operation by the summer of 1893, and the first ball at the hotel was held on February 28, 1894. Visitors swam in the warm waters while a string band entertained on the gallery. At 8:30, dinner was served in the dining hall with a dance following the meal. There were exotic animals and an ostrich farm, as well as domino and swimming parties. It was used in scenes in *The Immortal Alamo* (1911), by Star Films, the first film studio in San Antonio. The hotel was the film company's home, and in 1926, the property was again used in scenes for the movie *Wings*, the first Academy Award winner for best film in 1927. The commissioners and Hot Wells owner James Lifshutz have worked to start redevelopment of this fallen city treasure into a first-of-its-kind public park.

The postcard at top left reads, "I wish I was in Harley's place, don't you." Harley was just married, and his friend, a soldier at Fort Sam, was asked to write to a girl to share the news. The message shows the favor was accepted when a photograph of Alice Burnwell was shared. The old swinging bridge inspired stories for filming after a cowpoke got too pie-eyed at the hotel bar and fell off the bridge into the river. During World War I, the hotel and grounds were used to house officers and their families from Brooks Field. Part of the 10-acre pecan grove was transformed into a park and the Garden Café.

A man crosses Alamo Street some years before the summer of 1920, when the five-story Swearinger-McGraw building was razed. A letter from Alamo Flats dated January 16, 1896, mentions the building, but it is first described in a newspaper story on August 20, 1889. The named changed to the Alamo Hotel in December 1901. This hotel closed sometime in the mid-1940s. Another two-story Alamo Hotel was opened in the 1950s at 1327 North Alamo Street.

The Hotel Savoy opened on August 1, 1910, at 122 West Houston and Soledad Streets. It advertised "100 rooms, all with bath or toilet, telephones, steam heat, etc. $1.00 and up. "Cars from any station passed their entrance. In January 1948, the Savoy went into auction, and the entire furnishings of 64 rooms were sold. (Courtesy of the Texana Division, San Antonio Public Libraries.)

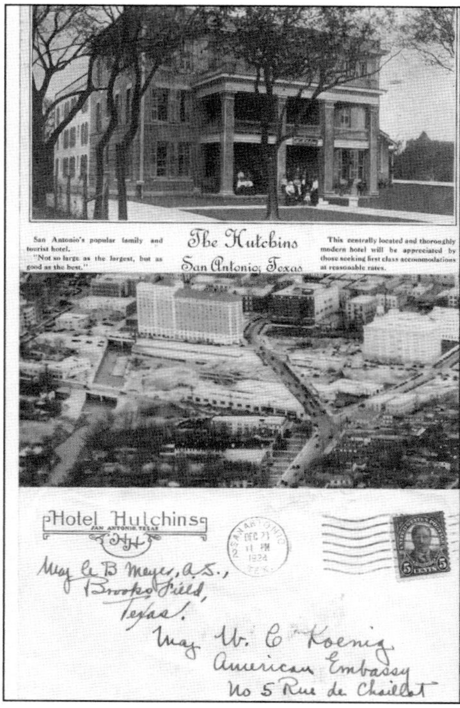

The Hutchins Hotel was located at 205 Garden Street, now South St. Mary's and East Nueva Streets. The hotel opened in the 1900s, and in October 1910, Mexican leader Francisco I. Madero came to San Antonio and stayed at the Hutchins. Here he transformed his notes into the Plan de San Luis Potosi, which called for the uprising and start of the Mexican Revolution. The hotel was razed at the end of 1958. Mayor Lila Cockrell proclaimed November 20, 1976, Madero Day, celebrating a leader who believed in democracy. This historical marker and a bronze statue of Madero, not shown, are located on the spot where the Hutchins Hotel once stood.

This photograph shows the Lopez grocery store, Rosita Bar, and two-story Jacalito Inn (closed in 1958). Based on the 1951 Chevy sedan's license plate, the photograph was taken in 1953 or 1954. The Navarro house was located on this street corner. Jose Antonio Navarro was one of two Texas-born signers of the Texas Declaration of Independence in 1836. Born in San Antonio and a Texas patriot until the end, Navarro passed away in his home at the age of 85 on January 13, 1871. The Casa Navarro State Historic Site was named a national historic landmark in 2017 and is a Texas Historical Commission property that is open to the public. (Courtesy of the San Antonio Conservation Society.)

The six-story, 220-room Lanier Hotel opened in 1916. The hotel was the White Plaza from 1941 to 1961 and the Travis Plaza Hotel from 1961 until it was razed in 1971. These four items are from the Lanier Hotel—an envelope with a commemorative Texas Centennial 1836–1936 postage stamp, a matchbook, a wooden dip ink pen painted olive green, and a postcard view of the lobby of the Lanier Hotel. (Left, Texana Division, San Antonio Public Libraries.)

This view from the Moore Building looks west on Houston Street. Across the street, the Hotel Maverick announced a reception for guests and the traveling public from 8:00 to 9:30 p.m. on Thursday, April 24, 1882, the night before it was open to the public, featuring a French menu from the popular caterer and steward Peter Loiselle. The Hicks building, on the right, had business slowly moving in during November 1896 as the building was completed. Marshall Hicks was mayor from 1899 to 1903.

Walking into the Maverick lobby, visitors saw men's and ladies' dining rooms, two small wine rooms, private rooms, offices, a bar, and a cigar stand. The kitchen was in the basement, and the staircase led to a parlor with fine furniture and a piano that was played often. Every floor had bathrooms, and the entire building was lit by gas. The hotel's rear galleries fronted the river. (Courtesy of the San Antonio Conservation Society.)

The Mission Hotel opened on Saturday, April 14, 1906. It was built by Silva Heimann and designed by Altlee B Ayres. More hotels were needed when the Southern Pacific Railroad station opened next door on February 1, 1903. Ayres and Heimann later designed the Heimann Hotel, which opened in 1909 at 188 North Medina Street, across from the International–Great Northern Railroad station. The Mission Hotel building is now the Conrad N. Hilton College of Hotel and Restaurant Management.

The Garden Hotel was built in the 1920s at 116 Garden Street, which later became St. Mary's Street. There was a three-story Navarro Hotel on West Commerce and Leona Streets in 1909; it caught fire in 1917, and 12–15 scantily clad persons narrowly escaped at 7:25 that Sunday morning. This Navarro Hotel was renovated and updated in the 1930s and advertised itself as "the Best Small Hotel in Bexar Co." The name changed to the O'Brien Hotel in 2003, and it has 39 beautifully decorated rooms. (Courtesy of the San Antonio Conservation Society.)

The most international place in San Antonio was at this north-facing corner block of Houston and West Commerce Streets. The block hosted the Mexico Hotel, Rio Grande Hotel, Nuevo Leon Hotel & Barber Shop, St. Louis tailors, Chicago bargain store, Texas portrait studio, Columbia dry goods store, City fish market, and International bakery, as shared on September 22, 1937, in the *San Antonio Light* by L.M. Bernal. Little was found, but on August 7, 1924, J.D. Olivares of the Nuevo Leon Hotel was arrested and booked for violation of the National Prohibition Act. The building was razed in 1973.

The Santa Monica Hotel is pictured in the summer of 1985. Since the 1990s, the hotel has been owned by R.K Hoover Commercial Contracting Inc., which is working with the Historic and Design Review Commission on this c. 1922 building. In 2018, favorable plans were ready for approval.

This panoramic view looks northwest from the courthouse and Main Plaza. In 1899, four streetcar companies were consolidated into one, the San Antonio Traction Company. The electric streetcar, which cost 5¢, is seen passing the front of the Southern Hotel. In 1917, the traction company merged with the San Antonio Gas & Electric Company to form San Antonio Public Service, today named City Public Service or CPS.

The *San Antonio Light* received a courteous invitation to attend the reopening of the Southern Hotel bar at 7:00 on Tuesday, October 21, 1884. The owners were W.C. Stillson and his assistant, Albert Friedrich. The paper reported, "This little gem of a saloon has been handsomely remodeled and fitted up very richly." The 20-year-old Friedrich went on to open the Buckhorn Saloon, today in its fourth location at 318 East Houston Street. (Courtesy of the San Antonio Conservation Society.)

At top right are the first electric streetlights on Houston Street. Passing the St. James Hotel are Gustav A. Duerler and Ferdinand Ludwig Herff on July 4, 1898. Herff, facing the camera, came to San Antonio from Germany after receiving his medical degree in 1843. He had a distinguished medical career in Texas and the Southwest and is honored with a Texas historical marker at the river level of the Nix Hospital, site of his former homestead. (Top left and bottom right, courtesy of the San Antonio Conservation Society.)

First called the Central Hotel when it opened around 1873, it was enlarged in 1882, then changed hands and reopened as the St. Leonard Hotel in the fall of 1883. The staff spoke German, French, Dutch, and Spanish. The first-class hotel was on the south side of Main Plaza, provided a post office, had cool airy halls and electric light, and was a popular resort for stockmen. (Courtesy of the San Antonio Conservation Society.)

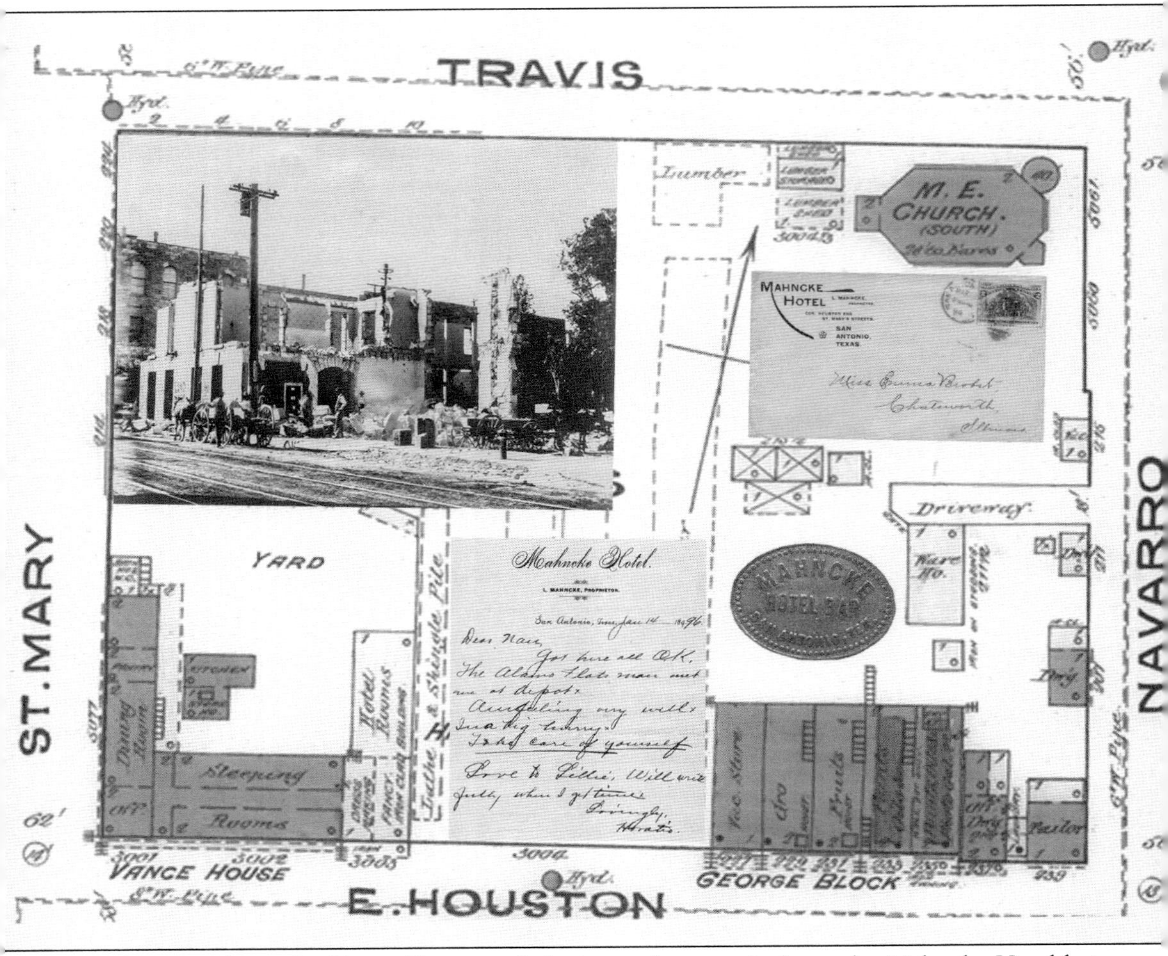

This map shows the Vance House, and the inset photograph shows the Mahncke Hotel being razed in 1908 for the construction of the Gunter Hotel. There is also a Mahncke Hotel envelope canceled with a 1492–1892 commemorative stamp. And last is a Mahncke bar token.

Eight

Now and Then

Looking north, women wash clothes next to the two-story French building with a view of San Fernando Church. John C. French was a dealer in groceries and a banker and constructed the office building in 1858. It served briefly as the courthouse and later housed San Antonio's First National Bank, whose president was George W. Brackenridge. William DeRyee, a chemist and photographer, maintained a studio in the building in 1859. DeRyee and Carl G. von Iwonski are credited with the "Main Plaza Surrender" and possibly this photograph. (Courtesy of the San Antonio Conservation Society.)

No date or information accompanied this view of San Antonio that was possibly taken by the Tobin Aerial Survey Company. The Plaza Hotel opened in 1928, and the 31-story Smith-Young Tower opened across the street on June 1, 1929. The Hutchins Hotel is at the wye in the street. Edgar G. Tobin was a World War I flying ace who started his aerial survey company after the war. It was considered the largest aerial mapping company in the world. Today, the Tobin Center is named in honor of the family's long-time contributions to San Antonio. (Courtesy of the Texana Division, San Antonio Public Libraries.)

Almost two years before a publisher was found for this book, the author requested that a friend, historian, and professional photographer capture this moment for the cover. Roughly 17 hotels and former hotels were captured this one night. At the bottom is the San Fernando Cathedral, where San Antonio's center of life and culture began in the 1700s. (Courtesy of Raul Medina III.)

The American Hotel was at Avenue C and Broadway. The hotel hosted a tacky party and dance on Valentines Day 1905. As reported in the *San Antonio Daily Light* on February 17, 1905, "The dining room was cleared and was ready to received 'tacks,' in their tacky attire. At 9 the orchestra called on the dance floor 20 couples. Liquid refreshments were served and the party carried on until it was announced, 'all good things must have an end,' and with that it was time to arrange the dining room for breakfast."

Located on the site of the American Hotel, now McCullough Avenue and Broadway Street, is public television station KLRN. The station began in September 1962 and has made it a mission to enrich the lives of people through the power of communication, providing quality programs and services that advance education, art, culture, and community. (Courtesy of Raul Medina III.)

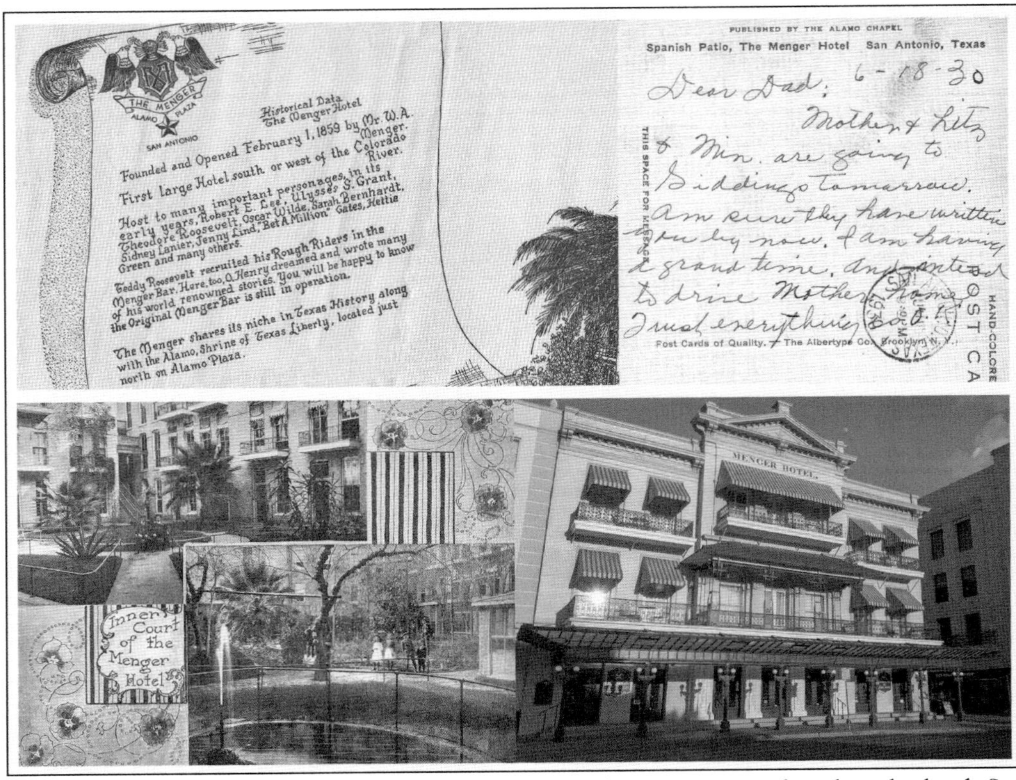

At the bottom left, this collage of the inner court of the Menger was found in the book *San Antonio through a Camera* (1903). The paper placemat at top left not only helped tablecloths but also offered dining guests Menger history and a possible souvenir of their visit. Sending a postcard (top right) home to say "I am having a grand time" was a way to share that one was thinking of this person. The Menger Hotel has two books readers can learn more from, *The History and Mystery of the Menger Hotel* by Docia Schultz William, and *The Haunted History of Old San Antonio* by Lauren M. Swartz and James A. Swartz.

Artist Shelby M. Rocca uses alternative photographic processes to create digital mimicry of tintypes, such as this image of the Crockett Hotel. (Courtesy of Shelby Rocca at shelbymrocca.com.)

RENDON
www.alrendon.com

At left on the sofa in the St. Anthony Hotel is Ernestine Seik, who worked at the hotel for almost 30 years, leaving in the mid-1980s. She had not returned since, so the author, right, set up this meeting with the St. Anthony's director of sales, Debbie Gonzales (center). Gonzales was formerly general manager at the Gunter Hotel when the hotel celebrated its 100th anniversary on November 20, 2009. (Courtesy of Al Rendon.)

The Old Spanish Trail 100th Anniversary, EL Tropicano Riverwalk Hotel November 14,15,16 2019

The historic Old Spanish Trail (OST) was named for the early Spanish explorers and missionaries who landed in Florida and along the Gulf of Mexico centuries ago. On November 1919, the Gunter Hotel became the headquarters for helping connect some of the oldest routes into a highway that spanned the nation from St. Augustine, Florida, to San Diego, California. The highway was completed in 1929. The OST will celebrate its 100th anniversary at the Tropicano Hotel with a three day event. The author will be present and will be a docent for a Houston Street walking tour.

Thank you for preserving San Antonio's rich history.

We are all connected in history in sometimes unexpected ways. While the author was taking photographs of William "Guillermo" Garza for an award he received, he invited the author to create historical prints for his restaurant, Guillermo's. Later the author learned his mother's grandparents were William's mother's godparents. Garza is seen here holding a Bexar Hotel brass key in front of the Bexar Hotel 1900 letter collage.

At the ribbon-cutting ceremony for the Maverick apartments on May 7, 2017, Stephanie Villa, also known as DJ Soulstairs, works her craft; Bob Reinhardt (right) wins the fast draw off the stormtrooper and says "Don't mess with Texas or Texas Bob." Downtown developer David Adelman spent $7 million renovating the Maverick building into 86 apartments and a restaurant and bar.

The word "maverick" got its start in 1800s San Antonio, when Samuel Maverick refused to brand his cattle. According to W.F. Strong, "In the world of words, it is a star: actor James Garner played Maverick in the TV western of the same name, Tom Cruise was Maverick in *Top Gun*, Senator John McCain's nickname was Maverick. The word means one who shuns custom, the lone wolf, one who blazes their own trail and is willing to go against the crowd, an independent thinker." This photograph, taken from the St. Anthony Hotel, shows a Hilton, a Marriott, two Hyatts, and the one and only Maverick.

The first Hyatt was opened as a motel near Los Angeles in 1954 by entrepreneurs Hyatt Robert von Dehn and Jack Dyer Crouch. In 1957, Hyatt became a corporation. Plans started for the Hyatt Regency Riverwalk Hotel around 1975, but by 1977, the company left the project and Stouffer Hotels took over. Hyatt came back, won the bid, and opened the Hyatt Regency Riverwalk in 1981.

The Hyatt Regency Riverwalk has one of the tallest atriums in the United States. Architect John Portman introduced the world's first modern atrium hotel, the Hyatt Regency in Atlanta, and later designed the 17-story atrium for the Hyatt Regency San Francisco. He said, "What do urban areas need the most? Space. Sidewalks and congested areas have a lot of anxiety and I wanted to create a release from that anxiety." The glass elevators, panoramic vista from the rooftop pool, 629 rooms, and the $26-million revitalization in 2003 have made the Hyatt Regency Riverwalk one of San Antonio's great hotels.

This aerial view shows the Marriott Rivercenter Hotel under construction. Even when it was completely bare, the views of San Antonio from its penthouse were breathtaking. The hotel opened in 1988. (Courtesy of the University of Texas–San Antonio Libraries, Special Collections from the Institute of Texan Cultures.)

Founders J.W. Marriott and wife Alice started their business with an A&W root beer stand in Washington, DC, in 1927. Marriott made a historic shift into the hotel business in 1957. In the late 1980s, Marriott began building the 38-story Marriott Rivercenter Hotel, the tallest building in San Antonio. (Courtesy of Raul Medina III.)

No information was provided with this photograph, although a Chevy Bel Air with a 1954 license plate can be seen parked on the Camden Street bridge. The wooden bridge on Newell Street runs in front of Samuels Glass Company, with the Preston Courts on the opposite side of the river. The San Antonio Brewing Association changed its named to Pearl Brewery company in 1952. Pabst Brewing took over in 1985, and in 2001, this historic plant was closed. (Courtesy of the University of Texas–San Antonio Libraries, Special Collections from the Institute of Texan Cultures.)

Its name still present on the brewhouse, the San Antonio Brewing Association was formed in 1887. The company was started by an investment group made up of local businessmen who were already involved in brewing on this site. In 2001, Silver Ventures purchased the 22-acre property, and after renovation, Aveda Institute opened its doors as the first Pearl tenant.

The Aztecs developed the ritual known as the Day of the Dead some 3,000 years ago. It was believed that one should not grieve the loss of beloved ancestors but instead celebrate their lives and welcome their spirits to the land of the living once a year. The Hotel Emma is named in honor of Emma Koehler. She ran the brewery after her husband, Pearl president Otto Koehler, died in 1914. A beautiful altar inside the Hotel Emma, pictured in November 2017, honors and celebrates the lives of Emma and Otto.

The Hotel Emma acquired the 3,700-volume library of Sherry Kafka Wagner, a San Antonio icon, novelist, historian, Harvard fellow, and cultural anthropologist. It is housed in one of the brewhouse's vaulted rooms. Hotel guests are allowed to browse the library using their room key 24 hours a day and check out books using the library's vintage card system. A copy of this book will be donated to the library.

The Central Trust Company Building opened in 1919 and was later renamed the South Texas Building. According to the plaque at top right, records for the site date to February 25, 1793, when the Spanish government granted the land to settler Matias del Rio. In 1982, a dedication ceremony was held to commemorate the building's restoration, with a time capsule placed in the cornerstone. In 2010, work started on the Home2 Suites by Hilton, and the hotel, with 128 studios and one-bedroom suites, opened in 2011.

Eighteen-year-old George Dullnig and his two brothers opened their wholesale and retail grocery business in 1864 on Commerce and Alamo Streets. With business prospering, George hired architect James Murphy to design a grand mercantile store. The resulting three-story building was an imposing landmark, constructed for an estimated $10,000 and opened in 1883. The building has hosted a variety of businesses and is now home to 17 tranquil, warmly appointed rooms and suites of the Riverwalk Vista Inn.

Construction of the new Brady Theatre started in April 1914, according to the *San Antonio Light*. Across the street is the historic two-story building that was Taliaferro's drugstore, Wagner's drugstore, Sommer's drugstore, and National Shirt Shop, and is now part of the Valencia Hotel. (Courtesy of the Marianist Archives, San Antonio.)

The Hotel Valencia River Walk opened in 2003 and was considered San Antonio's first boutique hotel. The hotel recently completed a $10-million renovation. "For the Hotel Valencia, we created a concept that blends Old World Spanish Colonial, to reflect San Antonio and its missions, with modern Mediterranean, to recall the building's Tuscan-style architecture and the hotel's namesake of Valencia, Spain," said Roteet designer Anja Majkic. "It's timeless and unique, all part of making the hotel a destination in itself."

In 1927, City Public Service added three additional floors to the building designed by architects Ayres and Ayres (bottom right). The location is historically significant because it is the original site of the Twohig House. *The Breadline Banker of St. Mary's Street* relates the story of John Twohig, a "romantic and historical sketch of the life, business man and a stalwart defender of San Antonio against many invasions during the pioneer days," wrote Gussie Scott Chaney in 1936. Because of its location and architectural design, the City Public Service Building is listed in the National Register of Historic Places. Fully restored, it is now the Drury Hotels Inn & Suites San Antonio Riverwalk. (Courtesy of the Marianist Archives, San Antonio.)

Kemmon Wilson opened the first Holiday Inn in Memphis, Tennessee, on August 1, 1952. Sixteen years later, on August 17, 1968, the 1,000th hotel was opened at Santa Rosa Street and Durango Avenue, now West César E. Chávez Boulevard. The Holiday Inn Downtown Riverwalk opened in the mid-1980s, where this plaque of Holiday Inn history is located.

In 1967, plans were made by Sam Barshop and his brother Phil to build three motor inns and expand a fourth. The very first La Quinta opened with 128 rooms on East Commerce Street just in time for the opening of Hemisfair. The second location was by the airport. The brothers had been in business for five years and already had five properties with a total of 295 rooms. The name is a Spanish term for a country villa. Today, this business that started in San Antonio has 870 hotels across the United States, Mexico, and Canada.

In 2018, the San Antonio Tricentennial Commission commemorated the 300th anniversary of the founding of the Mission San Antonio de Valero, the Presidio San Antonio de Bejar, and the city of San Antonio. Three centuries of San Antonio's diverse history and culture were honored and explored throughout the year through special events and initiatives. The Hilton Palacio del Rio hotel staff started the idea of lighting up the facade as a type of display board and have displayed the American flag, San Antonio Spurs pride, "Love," and this "300" and Christmas tree, to name a few.

The author stands in front of his two favorite San Antonio gems, the Hertzberg Clock (1878) and the Gunter Hotel. This photograph was conceived to honor family and friends who have helped him in his travels in this world and with the book. The suitcase, belonging to his aunt Sally Ramirez, is a tribute to her life as a maverick—a single woman who traveled the world. The author was inspired to add hotel labels from places he and his family have been to. He leaves this gift in gratitude for his blessings and the city he loves to future historians to continue to save the past while looking into the future.

Consistent with our mission to preserve history on a local level, this book was printed in South Carolina on American-made paper and manufactured entirely in the United States. Products carrying the accredited Forest Stewardship Council (FSC) label are printed on 100 percent FSC-certified paper.

MADE IN THE USA